Dear Edmond,

Thanks so much for buying **From The Other Side of The Tracks.** We hope you will it an interesting read. It's a unique insight into the final years of the now mythical *Continental Circus* and a story straight from the heart. It's the second book from WIDELINE Books but you may also be interested in our third, **Hailwood to Vincent,** as it has a similar racing focus. This is the second and final volume of our series on the BSA unit twins. Volume I covered the road bikes and won the accolade of *'Book of the year'* from Frank Westworth of Real Classic magazine and was dubbed *'A masterpiece'* by respected author Peter Henshaw, editor of Vintage & Classic Motorcycle.

Hailwood to Vincent is the long awaited companion volume and covers the little told competition history of the BSA A65/A50 twins and - as its title implies - covers the stories of the racers who made the bikes famous, as well as the technical aspects of the machines.

It is based around first-hand quotes and contributions from more than seventy five racers - including the BSA American works team of Dick Mann, Jim Rice, Dave Aldana and Don Emde – and is full of never seen before photos, as well as a year by year run down of the standout race results. Why not check it out at: **www.wideline.co.uk**

The story of the BSA A65 & A50 motorcycle 1962-1973

HAILWOOD to VINCENT

Volume II - The Racers

WIDELINE   Peter Crawford

Peter Crawford
WIDELINE Books - editor@wideline.co.uk

From The Other Side Of The Tracks

Life with a Racing Motorcyclist

WIDELINE

First published in Great Britain in 2018 by:
Amazon Kindle Direct ASIN : B07CJ6F32Q

Second Edition published 2021 by;
WIDELINE Ltd - www.wideline.co.uk: ISBN 9781838133610

Whilst every effort has been made to ensure the accuracy of this book, opinions expressed herein are those of the author and do not necessarily represent the views of persons represented.

Photographs used draw extensively on the Peter Horton archive but also include images by Len Thorpe, Brian Kelly, Maurice Bulle, Chris Morgan and Steve Powell. In each case every effort has been made to contact the originator of photographs used.

A CIP catalogue record of this book is available in the British Library ISBN 9781838133610

Printed in Malta by

From The Other Side Of The Tracks

Life with a Racing Motorcyclist

Sue Horton

Introduction and Acknowledgements

It has taken over 15 years from the germination of an idea and the production of the first few hundred pages of rough and ready text to get a finished book out into the light. That first draft had languished in the bowels of my computer for more than a decade when I asked my late writer friend Peter McManus what he thought of it. He liked it and said it was a tale that needed to be told. Encouraged, I set about completing the project.

There are many hundreds of biographies by ex-professional sports persons, but few by their long suffering partners. I hope this helps tip the balance a little. It's a love story with motorcycle racing as its backdrop. And its about a love of racing. It's a tale of sex, racing and rock and roll, and about a time that is now passing into history. I can't take anything entirely seriously so it is written with a comedic bent. It's about success and failure, love and heartache, fun and adventure, and of two lives, I hope, well lived. It may make you laugh and cry.

I would like to thank my indefatigable typist and sternest critic, Clive; and our long-time friend, arch-journalist Chris Carter, for his sage advice that we should get an editor involved. '*He will make it a better book,*' said Chris. Thanks also then to Richard Skelton for being that man, although he has removed some sex scenes (probably for the best!), and a heavenward nod to Peter McManus for the stimulating advice and encouragement which lit the blue touch paper. Finally, and most importantly, thank you to every member of the cast in this production. Life's treasure I call them.

Sue Horton 2017

Foreward by Jon Ekerold
1980 350cc World Champion

I'm not sure when or where I first met Clive, but it was at a race meeting, that much I do know. We were brothers-in-arms, so to speak, in the sense that we were both trying to live our dream of making a living from what we loved doing most in life, racing motorcycles. We belonged to a group of young men who, together with our families, toured around Europe from one race meeting to another hoping to be spotted by one of the factories, something that would have made two major changes to our lives. Firstly, it would have ensured financial security, never a bad thing, and secondly, it would mean the chance to challenge for world titles, something everyone who ever slung a leg over a saddle dreamed of doing.

We were what were known as privateers, and we belonged to a group called the continental circus. Our idyllic life style looks oh so romantic in hindsight, but at the time it was a hard grind, as well as bloody dangerous. Clive concentrated on the smaller capacity classes, which, if anything, made his job even harder, but he was one of the top men and he earned a great deal of respect for his hard riding and determined style.

Reading Sue's book was a revelation, besides being side-splittingly funny. She describes life from a perspective very few have seen, that of wife and companion to one of the crazy, but lucky men who chose this path in life. How fortunate she was to find herself in that happy situation. There were trials and tribulations to be sure, but at the end of the day, how many people can look back at a youth so thoroughly misspent? If you judge success in life in terms of financial gain, then none of us amounted to much, but when I tell you that all the money in the world could never have bought what we experienced in our youth, then you had better believe it. I mean, come on, how many people could fill a book with so many delightful stories and tales if all they ever did was make a lot of money? Life is a tapestry of experiences, some good and some not so good, and that is what makes it interesting.

I want to thank Sue and Clive for enriching all our lives, not only for helping to make those years so special, but also for now taking the time to share their story with us. This great tale takes you to the very heart of what we all experienced, and it makes for fascinating reading.

Foreward by Peter McManus
(1924-2017)

I first met Sue Horton several years ago while working on a follow up to my book *Derbyshire's Motorcycle Maestros*. I was interviewing her husband, Clive, about his racing career, but I soon realised Sue had a unique and fascinating story to tell in her own right. She impressed me as a person and the rough manuscript of this book which she tentatively showed me was written with such wit, humour and verve that I encouraged her to continue to work on it and to publish it. This is the result.

From the age of 18 she has been Clive's guide, philosopher-friend, and equal partner throughout his motorcycling career and beyond, and as far as I am aware this is the first book about the world of motorcycle racing written from an entirely feminine point of view.

This truly is a view 'From the Other Side of the Tracks', but it is not just a book about racing. Sue and Clive's life together is an ongoing love story and Sue has written about the development and the ups and downs of their relationship with a candour never before attempted in a book about motorbikes. It is a book for men and for women, for motorcyclists, yes, but for non-bikers too. Enjoy it.

Clive always said I had a good set of pins

It shouldn't have been this hard

It can be a fraught business being the girlfriend, wife, or mother of a motorcycle racer. Sometimes it is difficult to know if you are dealing with an adrenaline junkie or a madman. Maybe it's both. Certainly, when it comes to the priorities in his life, you come way down the list and certainly after his motorcycles.

We women, of course, are not encumbered, as men are, with testosterone. It is therefore impossible to see things entirely from their point of view. Nevertheless, I say go along for the ride. You never know where a racing life might take you. Above all enjoy the journey, join in and take part, even on those days when you just want to bash some sense into him.

These racing types come as a package. If you fall for one, you can't have the man without the racing. You can't pick and choose. And I have seen over the years that if you stand back from the racing you will be missing out on some exciting adventures and the relationship will not stand the test of time.

It can be an exotic life too, but the chances of that are few and far between. Clive had been racing for a season, that's March to October, before I started going out with him in October 1969. He had travelled around the circuits with his cousin, Peter, who also raced a motorbike. In fact, it had been Peter who had inspired Clive's racing ambitions in the first place by taking him along to Mallory Park in Leicestershire to watch greats such as Mike Hailwood, Giacomo Agostini, and local hero John Cooper.

Clive claims he wasn't overly interested in the racing at first, but really enjoyed travelling on the back of Pete's 600cc Norton Dominator. Pete then took up racing on an ex-GPO BSA Bantam, taking Clive along as 'gofer', and after watching Pete perform for a couple of years he decided he could do better. Quite how he knew this is another matter because, as far as I'm aware, he had never even ridden a motorcycle at this point in his life, but his instinct was not entirely wrong.

And when I came into his life he quickly persuaded me to take my driving test and to buy a van, and with my second-hand Vauxhall Viva van, resplendent in a fetching shade of powder blue, I became his permanent travelling companion and partner. Some of you may remember those rather boxy 5cwt HA Vivas. They had their body seams on the outside. Why the marketing department let that one through God alone knows, but this was the dawn of the 1970s and anything was possible. Man had just walked on the moon after all!

When we went racing in that first season the front wheel of his little BSA used to rest on the van's handbrake, so it was all a bit cramped, but once the bike was unloaded we could camp overnight in it, and in the morning, with condensation dripping from the roof, (there is a good deal of vigour to be worked off at that age), I would tidy up and make breakfast while the bike was ministered to in the open air. As well as the van, you see, I had other things to offer with which Peter could not compete. One being the obvious, and the other was that I could cook a bit!

Back then all the cooking was done on a two-burner Calor gas camping stove. Ah the memories! After starting by cooking the basics, like tea, fried bacon and boiled eggs, I progressed to making lunches comprising fish fingers, mashed potatoes, parsley sauce, and peas. All on that rotten little stove. Clive was so impressed he started inviting his racing friends over to share this sumptuous fare.

One of the first couples to join us for lunch in the paddock was Leigh and Janice Notman, who were most surprised that lunch was rather more than basic hot dog and beans. Before they got a van, Leigh and Janice would travel to race meetings on a motorbike and sidecar with the race bike strapped on the sidecar platform. Now that was impressive! Clearly, they displayed the combination of determination and insanity needed for this racing business.

Another person I remember from day one was a charming, friendly Lincolnshireman called Neil Tuxworth. I remember Neil went out of his way to make me feel at ease on my first day in this strange new environment, and for that I'll always be grateful. Clive also got on well with Neil, and we are firm friends with him to this day.

Never, in my most random thoughts did I ever see myself actually driving around a race circuit. That was the riders' job wasn't it? But at our first ever race meeting together, at a very chilly Snetterton circuit in early 1970, that is exactly what happened. The track was covered in a dusting of March snow and everyone with a vehicle was asked to drive round the circuit, lap after lap, to melt it so the idiot competitors could race their bikes. It worked too!

Then, after breakfast, and when the riders' entries and licences had been checked, and technical inspection of the race machines had taken place, practice duly commenced, and I received my next promotion. Having already completed the tests for bimbette, van driver and cook, I was now… Tad-ah! stopwatch operative!

At first I was little more than a baffled spectator, standing by a pit wall, watch in hand, trying to spot my rider coming round Coram Curve in a fuzzy white blizzard. It was snowing again and I concluded I was witnessing utter madness. Surely to God, they must draw a line somewhere? I came to realise they never do. After several years being part of multitudinous crazy situations, I

3

concluded these racer types sometimes need outside help to save them from themselves. Anyway, day one at Snetterton was a big eye-opener.

OK, so the racing life was not entirely as I had envisaged, but it was exciting and I was thrilled when Clive won his race. I absolutely loved it. It was fun and and different, and I knew a new and significant chapter in my life had begun. As we made our way home after that first race meeting together I decided it had been well worth all the trouble I had gone to getting Clive to go out with me. I didn't think I was a bad catch, but by golly, he had made it hard work. Just like when he was out on the race track, he definitely took some hunting down!

Clive had three jobs at the time, one of which was as a van driver for a Derby firm called Coussins Hardware, and his role was to deliver stock and move items between a string of retail shops owned by the company. I worked at the Coussins' Alvaston branch in the south-east of the city, and had done since I had been asked to leave Shelton Lock Secondary School nearby, aged just 14. My crime? Fighting. In my defence I will say that although I did finish the fight I did not start it! The problem was I had a bit of previous, if you know what I mean, and if you're marked down as a bit of a rebel you're unlikely to get a fair trial.

Never mind, it wasn't the end of the world. Despite being fairly bright at school I was happy enough to quit and start earning some money. My Mum, Kate, was a well-respected supervisor at Coussins and as I was already working for the firm as a Saturday girl, promotion to full-time employment was something of a formality. By the time I was 17 I was an old hand.

Clive had attended the same school as me but he was two years ahead and, shall we say, not in the top class. Consequently, most of the kids he hung around with were not the brightest bulbs on the Christmas tree so I can't say I really noticed him there.

But there's something to be said for late development and a few years later I noticed him alright, and I really used to look forward to our visits from this long-haired hippy. With his shoulder-length hair he could have been cast in the lead role in Jesus Christ Superstar, or at least been his stunt double! Sadly, he didn't seem to take any interest in me, other than in a professional sense.

He only worked for the firm on Saturdays as he had a proper job in the week as some kind of apprentice metal analyst, I understood, so to gain his attention, and to try to get him to 'Be My Baby' (© Ronettes 1964), my Saturday skirts got shorter and shorter, until I was wearing only a belt!

One day he turned up on his moped, a dark blue Italian thing that he'd rescued from scrap and rebuilt in his bedroom. I pretended to admire it, coquettishly touching it, running my fingers along the fuel tank and asking him for a ride. He whizzed up the local bypass with me sitting on the rack over the rear mudguard. It took ages, but I made out I was rather thrilled, but actually I was just chilled to the bone after four miles of a cold draft blowing up my skirt. But after that brief excitement, I received no extra attention. I guess he thought I was just a bit daft.

My next opportunity to impress was when he gave me a lift in his van to one of the other shops. I kissed him for the lift and he thought it was 'rather nice'. Success! On another occasion soon afterwards I managed to persuade him to give me a lift home, and I kissed him some more (quite a bit actually), and I invited him in. My Mum and Dad were out, so one thing led to another and by the time he left he was pretty well 'magnetised', shall we say? I was making progress.

I can't help thinking that it should not have been such hard work. Clive must be a simpleton when it comes to the opposite sex. He claimed later that it was a result of having been rejected. Rejection can be hard on men and putting his metallurgist's cap on, he explained it thus: Metal, when it is heated to red then plunged into cold water, becomes harder. After each rejection, one's heart gets progressively harder, until the point is reached whereupon it is so hard, it is impenetrable! Fanciful, or a brilliant analogy?

According to Clive, several months before I started making my big effort to gain his attention, I was going out with another boy and unwittingly became part of the hardening process. (Do try to keep it clean! This is a metallurgical metaphor, not a physiological one). He says I complained to him that my boyfriend would not take me to the travelling fair which had come to town, and he offered to take me instead. Apparently I curled my lip and said 'You? Phnerr!' (if that is how you spell a sneer). Cue hissing sound and clouds of steam. I can recall nothing of this incident, so of course he might have made it all up! If true, however, it explains his standoffishness, I suppose.

In the winter of 1969/70 we would often spend our evenings in the cellar bar of the Berni inn, on Irongate in Derby, sharing half a pint of lager and lime making it last all night. It must have cost the best part of a shilling too, being a bit of a posh gaff. We listened to the juke box playing 'our song', Serge Gainsbourg and Jane Birkin's Je T'aime. I'm glad it wasn't the other popular tune at the time, although it was a close call; Lee Marvin's Wandering Star. Not for the last time, luck was on our side.

Promotion

I became a very competent timekeeper after a couple of race meetings, and an upgrade to two stopwatches meant every lap could be recorded instead of alternate ones. To do this the stopwatches need to be mounted on a clipboard and pressed simultaneously. Lap timing is not as easy a job as you might imagine. Clive can't do it as he gets distracted far too easily. You have to concentrate and keep cool and calm, even when the race is getting super exciting. All that, of course, was in the olden days when timekeeping was a skilled job. Nowadays it is all done by electronics and computers, and info is often beamed directly to the rider's dashboard.

Back in 1970 we were club racing on a really basic motorcycle, and I guess the races and meetings we were part of with the Bantam Racing Club were no big deal in the grand scheme of things. But we had many good experiences in our first year going racing together.

Hey, we were living the high life. Between us we were on more than 30 quid a week, so we could afford to go crazy and visit Pancake Paradise (and park on the street outside) in London's Soho on trips to Brands Hatch, or take in the sights and delights of Llantwit Major on a visit to the Llandow race circuit in Wales. I am being a little ironic. There was actually little of interest to us there, unless you really wanted to see the odd bit of brown scum on the beach, flotsam deposited as a result of the Torrey Canyon disaster in 1967.

Llandow was a bit of a rough, backwoods track and not really worth a visit, unless you are addicted to risking your life every weekend. On weekdays sheep grazed on the green bits and their 'doings' on the tarmac stretches proved highly detrimental to tyre adhesion.

Once, after racing at Brands, we did a tour of the Kent cinque ports and had a little holiday. Oh, the exciting life of a road racer's bimbo.

One day my git of a new boyfriend borrowed my little van and brought it back somewhat mangled. He was steaming down the outside of a lane of slow-moving traffic and someone was following behind, but when Clive indicated right and turned into a junction the poor bloke in his slipstream was caught completely by surprise! The chap made every effort to avoid hitting my van and I have to give him top marks for that, but his speed was too high for this manoeuvre and he smashed straight into the right side of the Viva, pushing it onto the pavement.

The bloke said he thought Clive was just overtaking and never in a million years did he expect him to turn at that speed. Big mistake. Little did he know the twerp he was following raced a motorbike. Besides, he was following far too closely which is always super risky. This sort of behaviour is common on race tracks, where cars and bikes slipstream each other for extra speed - why else would these barmpots do it? - and even F1 drivers hit one another up the backside on occasions and they are the supposedly the best drivers in the world. What chance did an everyday bloke stand?

Clive was awfully embarrassed about bringing my knackered van back, but I handled it pretty dispassionately I like to think. No big drama. I like to think perhaps I inherited a bit of this cool from my mum.

Now when it came to spilled breadcrumbs, my mum would run around flapping her arms, but give her a five-star calamity to deal with and she would handle the situation with utter calm and aplomb. It can sometimes be very hard to understand that kind of personality.

The van was written off but I soon discovered, at just 18 years of age, that I had innate negotiating skills. After much haggling with my insurance company, I arranged to keep the van and get paid its write-off value too.

By that time I was working in the car trade, and I managed to acquire all the parts needed to fix the Viva at a very good price. Clive, for his part, carried out the repairs, and it was after we got it back on the road, with its driver's door and offside front wing resplendent in red oxide primer, that we made our cinque ports trip. I can sense you asking why the heck the cinque ports? Well, Clive's mind wasn't totally bunged up with motorbikes, there was a couple of brain cells spare for cultivating an interest in history and geography. And what else can you do on the Kent coast?

We could see France from the parapet of Dover castle too, and Europe is where he really wanted to be - racing a motorcycle and making a precarious living on the continental circus. Yep, he wanted to run away and join the circus, but we're talking motorcycle Grands Prix, not the big top!

A dirty weekend

After a few days sight-seeing around the castles of Kent, it was time to return home, and that is when I turned the Viva over on the M1 as a result of a blow-out and finished the poor old thing off once and for all. As I have mentioned, it was still in red oxide and not fully recovered from its last traumatic experience, and now it was my turn to knock some corners off it.

You often hear racers saying that a crash happens in slow motion and I can confirm that it does. I suppose the mind hits hyperdrive as the adrenalin is pumped in and you are processing information so fast that real time seems like a slo-mo action replay. Bang! The steering wheel was wrenched from my hands. We lurched left into the middle lane. Then there was a 180 degree roll onto the roof. The van then slid across the slow lane and finally came to rest upside down on the hard shoulder. All without hitting another vehicle. How lucky was that?

We were not wearing seat belts, so we ended up in a rather unattractive, crumpled and inverted heap on the inside of the roof. Miraculously we were pretty much unscathed, although Clive was complaining about a cold liquid sensation running down his back. Actually, that may have been up his back! Anyway, as a crash veteran he had the presence of mind to tell me not to touch the ignition just in case, in our confusion, I turned it the wrong way, released a flow of high voltage current and started a fire. That would have been a nuisance!

Clive also recalls the crash in high definition slow-motion. Looking through the passenger window he saw lorries and cars bearing down on us and getting closer and closer as we lurched left and tumbled over, while saying calmly to himself, 'Ah, I see, so this is how a motorway pile-up starts.'

A kindly lorry driver stopped and got me out somehow, before sitting me in his cab and calming me down. He was a good man. Thank you, wherever you may be. Clive slithered out of the passenger window aperture and I saw him inspecting the damage to his bike. Priorities! He was also continuing to query the cold liquid sensation he was feeling on his back. Was it blood from a ruptured spleen? Spilled battery acid? Petrol, that could burst into flames at any moment? Eek! Nope, it was goo from a broken box of eggs.

The motorway police arrived and an officer handed me the van's first aid kit, which he'd picked up off the road somewhere. I was in shock. but I was amused by the irony. An ambulance crew arrived next and were insistent I go to hospital for a check up. I did not want to comply, thinking Clive needed their attention more than me. He had a bit of gravel in his eye and a terminally eggy vest. In the end they took us both to Luton General, conveniently failing to mention we would eventually be invoiced for this service. More of that later, but at least we were soon inside with access to a telephone so we could call for help.

Both sets of parents later arrived and they gathered our goods, chattels and racing accoutrements together and loaded everything into the Coussins Hardware van. It's great having reliable, resourceful parents to call upon in one's hour of need, and we were forced to concede that our mums and dads could be quite handy when we thought about it.

Clive's parents Reg and Ivy didn't understand for one moment why he wanted to risk life and limb racing motorbikes, but they were always very supportive of his racing career. But I'm afraid my Mum and Dad were not at all happy when Clive and I got together. Going off for weekends, sleeping in the back of a van and hanging out with bikers, what was I thinking! And even before I went racing they got in a right hump when I told them I was off to London with my new racer boyfriend to attend a swanky motorcycle prize-giving event. Worse still, we were planning to stay overnight together in a hotel in Russell Square.

This event took place at a very early stage in our relationship, and my mum and dad were not pleased about it at all, but I had turned eighteen by then and there was not much they could do about it. I was going and that was that, but as a result my parents' concerns about my unfortunate choice of boyfriend continued to increase and I did not talk to them for nearly a week.

As I have mentioned, my mum, Kate, worked for the same hardware company as me, and as a branch supervisor she thought Clive was a bit of a jack the lad. He was unreliable, she said, and she didn't 'get' this racing thing at all. But on the positive side... sort of... if you stretched a point, she thought he was trustworthy... well, -ish. She was not at all impressed by his serial forgetfulness in having once failed to pass on a vital message to the supervisor at another branch. 'I had to tell him fourteen times!' she said. Actually, I can see where she went wrong. Her overbearing method bored him senseless, to the point where just switched off.

'He has the moustache of a villain and a cad,' she added unnecessarily. 'Yeah, so what? So does Dad,' I countered. Personally, I thought it was more fighter pilot-style or Graham Hill-like, but different folks have different strokes, so I let it pass. My Dad Jack's opinion of him was even lower. Bound to be so, I guess. Let's face it, I was his daughter, and he knew how men thought and operated, or so he thought. Furthermore, he disliked motorcyclists intensely, considering them the dregs of humanity, even though my brother John owned a pretty little 100cc Bianchi.

I couldn't explain that Clive was different. That he was so different it had been me who had seduced him! How could I?

I hope too, he never guessed, or imagined, that when he and mum went out to the pub, Clive and I would get up to gymnastics on my single bed in my little room. If they failed to go to the pub we would canoodle in the lounge, away from their gaze as they never used the room themselves. It was only used for best as they preferred to watch the telly in the kitchen/diner. So we'd get up to a bit of snogging listening to Andy Williams, The Four Seasons or Elvis, and once they'd finally retired to bed we would wrestle quietly on the sheepskin hearth rug to a bit of reggae music. It has an excellent rhythm for that kind of thing.

In the early hours of the morning I would let Clive out and he would walk home in the dark, a journey of about a mile. Well, he walked most of the way but he would sprint for 50 yards past the cemetery, a place which always gave him the creeps. Now this always struck me as a bit odd because he had another part-time job cutting the grass in a graveyard, trimming neatly around all the marble monoliths and victorian gravestones. But I guess that was OK because it was always in the hazy evening light of a summer's day. I suppose the pitch blackness of the early hours sets the imagination racing and adds a smidgeon of terror.

I should mention that Clive was going through a tough time at this point as his younger brother Jim had just been diagnosed with leukaemia and the poor lad did not have long to live. Understandably, Clive struggled with the unfairness of his brother's life being brought to an end at just 16 and I tried to provide a shoulder to cry on. I hope it helped. How his Mum, Ivy, coped with it I really can't imagine. Most parents would change places with their child in these circumstances but, of course, that's not an option.

Where were we? Oh yes. The Bantam Racing Club's annual dinner, dance and prize-giving was to take place at the Cafe Royal in Piccadilly, a rather posh gaff opened in 1865 by a bankrupt French wine merchant. It was very swish indeed, and in days of yore its well-to-do owners had enjoyed the patronage of clients of the calibre of Winston Churchill, DH Lawrence, Oscar Wilde, George Bernard Shaw, Virginia Wolfe, and Noel Coward. The list of the great and good goes on, and in the winter of 1969 it was extended by two more famous names - Clive and me.

Before we went, Clive was tipped off by one or two of his racing pals about the high cost of drinks at this establishment and the consensus seemed to be take your own booze, buy the first one to get a glass, then use that to drink your own stuff. Clive took a briefcase full of beer and he looked especially incongruous staggering around with the thing wearing a lounge suit and a frilly shirt. These were the de rigour garments of the day, along with a pair of Lionel Blairs (flared trousers). Many men dressed foppishly in the flower power era and, rather surprisingly, didn't get duffed up for it either!

Clive was awarded a two-inch high pewter tankard, suitably inscribed as a reward for a magnificent 'Third Place, Novice Race, Cadwell Park'. We still have it somewhere, saved for sentimental reasons, unlike most of his trophies which have long-since been consigned to the tip. Later on, dinner and prize-giving over, the Cafe Royal's large, round dining tables were moved aside exposing the dance floor, and while the boogying got underway, we grabbed ourselves a drink from the bar and bagged a side table with some friends.

Now then, when you have brains smaller than your balls it is possible to have ideas outside the box, as it were. Clive emptied the contents of his briefcase and placed the bottles in the centre of the table for everyone to share. So it wasn't long, of course, before a group of chunky waiters and even chunkier bouncers surrounded the table and stood, legs splayed, arms akimbo and with knitted eyebrows, scowling fiercely.

'You aren't allowed to bring your own refreshments, SIR' were the words hissed in his shell-like by the menacing maitre'd. Bold as brass he came back with, 'OK then, get me a half of lager please.' 'Sorry SIR, one will have to fetch one's own, I'm afraid.' Now we knew where we stood. Brass neck does not generally cut it in the big smoke where it was invented.

Never mind, after a bit of enthusiastic rockin' and a rollin', twistin' and a shoutin', a shakin' and a shapin', the shame and embarrassment fell away and we felt marvellous.

Not a smooching though? Clive thought we were a bit too sweaty for that. How odd. You would think a bloke would love an excuse to rub himself all over a girl. Not Clive. He would much rather writhe around impersonating Mick Jagger!

The Cafe Royal closed in 1976. Not down to us I'm sure, although the Bantam Club was declared persona non grata after that night (or is it persona au gratin!). It has since been converted into a very swanky hotel.

15

The end of the line

A fter its ordeal on the M1, my powder blue and red oxide HA Viva had drawn its final breath, even Paul Daniels, (substitute David Nixon or Paul McKenna depending on your age group) could not have bought it back to life this time.

Posing with the Jack Machin-framed 125cc AS1 Yamaha

But the biggest shock of the whole event was receiving an invoice for the ambulance. I was outraged, but no amount of shouting and snarling down the phone would get it to disappear. We had to pay it. If I remember correctly it was only 30 quid, but that was a lot of money to us then - more than our spending money for a month! If the ambulance people had been up front with us we would have walked to the hospital in Luton. The b*****ds!

Negotiating with the insurance company was the usual nightmare. They tried to knock the price down as is their standard practice, saying the van wasn't in good condition. 'Yes,' we agreed, 'but only because it's been stored outside in a scrap yard for two months waiting for you to get round to looking at it!' I didn't give them an inch, because I felt I was dealing with professional villains.

We needed another van so we visited John Cooper who, at that time, was a top level racing star to say the least. His day job was running his petrol station and garage in Derby. We told him we had been looking at a Morris Minor van at 125 quid and his typically pithy response was, 'I don't know where you can buy a decent set of wheels and brakes for that money, never mind have a van attached to them. Hang on, I'll find you something.' And with that he ambled off.

Waiting around on his forecourt we eyed a two-tone green, ex-Qualcast Bedford van. 'Cor, wouldn't it be nice if we could afford that?' said Clive. I could tell he was smitten. Qualcast was a world famous and well respected lawnmower manufacturer and foundry based on Victory Road, Derby, and we knew it was a former Qualcast vehicle as the company name was still faintly visible behind swirly sandpaper scars on its flanks, giving its provenance away.

John returned, took us over to it and said: 'How about this one for 185 quid?' Done!

John is, and always will be, a bit of a philanthropist, always ready to give someone a hand up, and never a kick down. Occasionally this has cost him dear, but he is still the same, still there offering folk a hand up. The world would be a better place if there were more people like him. Be like John Cooper!

With the insurance money and our combined holiday pay we had just about enough to buy the Qualcast van and have a week's holiday in Cornwall in it. Luxury? We didn't know the meaning of the word. Wow! It was a great van with sliding cab doors and a nifty three-speed column change gearbox. Actually, it was a bit of a bugger to drive and only Clive and I truly mastered it. It was like Roy Rogers' horse Trigger!

Clive sprayed over the signwriting remnants and spruced up the front panel with a few cans of red Humbrol paint, so it became two-tone green with two bright red panels and a big red nose. No really, it looked great! In Cornwall we kept getting moved on by car park attendants or stick-wielding farmers as we were neither willing nor able to pay any parking or camping fees. We didn't return to England's most south-western county for over 30 years, but now we can't keep away. The car park sharkery has not changed in the interim, except that the prices have gone up exponentially. Yes, time spent in Cornwall is never regretted. What better than a shared Cornish pasty and two half pints of beer for lunch!

Back then we were living high on the hog, feasting on breakfasts cooked on our Calor gas stove, lazing about reading books, and splashing out on cinema tickets to see Easy Rider and Butch Cassidy and the Sundance Kid. Simply living the dream.

Let's get serious

At the end of the 1971 season, concluding that Bantam racing was a class that no one would ever take seriously, we decided to sell the BSA and move on. The Bantam was a simple beginner's machine with a three-speed gearbox. Throughout the 1960s, Bantam racing had been, in many ways, a delightful choice for dedicated enthusiasts, tinkerers, and even talented engineers in search of a challenge, and for would-be racers with a burning desire for excitement but very little cash. But now the class had had its day. The little Beesa had been perfect for Clive at the start of his career, but now we were in the 1970s, man. Yep, time to move on. You dig?

What next? Well, we bought a 125cc Yamaha AS1 from a young lad's insurance company. Clive's dad serendipitously picked the exact machine we needed when he knocked the poor kid off it in a traffic accident. And then we got to buy the bike. Now obviously this was not part of any plan, but at the time it did seem like divine providence. The damaged machine was gutted for its engine and all serviceable remains were sold for spares. Team Horton was getting serious! Before continuing I should mention the youth wasn't hurt at all, and only his bike was sacrificed to our cause. Maybe it put him off riding the things for life!

We engaged fellow Bantam racer, John Smith, welder, pipe bender and altogether thoroughly nice man, to make us a chassis. John worked as a welder at Lotus, and had helped make F1 cars for Jim Clark and Graham Hill. But before he could get started on our frame he had to get better.

Better? Ah yes, he had crashed his Bantam in a race at Cadwell Park the same day we shook hands on the deal. The crash was a bad 'un as John elected to stay on board after losing control of his machine, hanging on as it took off across the grass heading for an earth bank. Earth banks were used quite extensively at race circuits in those days to protect spectators from bikes and debris flying hither and yon.

Now then, in the few moments between leaving the nice smooth race surface and hitting the bank we enter a slow-mo sequence, but during it the rider is thinking faster than lightning. 'Oh flip, I'm heading for that solid wall of earth! I know, I have an idea! I will jump off the bike the precise moment it touches the bank. I will then be thrown clear and I can deal with the relatively minor consequences as they occur.' All fine in theory, but in practice, with man and machine covering around 100 feet per second, all that usually happens is SPLAT! John's bike rammed the bank and both of his femurs snapped when they made contact with his handlebars as his body weight carried him onwards.

We visited John in the hospital at Louth, where he was plastered up and suspended by all manner of mechanical contraptions, just like you might see in a comedy film or cartoon. He was sedated but came to sufficiently to tell us, 'Don't worry, I will still be able to make your frame in time for next season.' I tell you what, these racer types, always have their focus on racing, even when semi-conscious and decidedly bleary-eyed.

John was later transferred to hospital in Norwich, nearer his home, and it was there, in November 1971, that we visited him again. He was making progress and confident in his recovery. We drove the 140 miles back to Derby in freezing fog, in the pitch black dead of night. We couldn't see a hand in front of our faces, icicles were forming on the wing mirrors. It was horrendous, not least because we had to drive with the sliding doors clicked wide open so we could see the road. I, on the passenger side, gave guidance to prevent us running up the curb, while Clive caught glimpses of white lines to his right. We don't seem to get fog as dense as that these days do we?

When John was finally out of hospital and up on his two dodgy legs, we returned to Norwich once again to help him with the construction. The fundamental dimensions for the bike were basically copied from a frame made by Spondon Engineering for Granby Motors (I don't think Jack Glover, the boss of Granby's Ilkeston shop, ever forgave Clive for that!), and the frame tube layout was copied from the brilliant 350cc Yamsel, devised and deployed to such magnificent effect by John Cooper.

The Eurovision Song Contest was ending on the TV as we left John's house in the dark. The New Seekers' Beg, Steal or Borrow had just been pipped into second place by a barnstorming ballad sung in French by a beautiful Greek singer representing Luxembourg, who lived in Germany. You can't get much more international than that!

We finished the bike off at home and it looked truly beautiful - all powder blue and purple metal flake. Groovy baby! The only trouble was when it was raced it juddered something rotten in the corners and was truly horrible to ride, according to Clive. Not so bad in the wet, where one rides a little slower, but a pig in the dry. Too ignorant to understand the nature of the problem, we soldiered on.

So when racer Jack Machin offered to sell us his home-built rolling chassis we snapped it up. It was a tried and tested piece of engineering and in a test ride at Cadwell Park Clive absolutely flew. We were smiling once again and brimming with optimism. Things went forwards quite quickly from then on.

Our first trip aboard had been with our friend from Bantam days, Neil Tuxworth. He and Clive agreed to share a 250cc Suzuki in a six-hour endurance race at Zandvoort in Holland. Neil at that time had a paranoid fear of crossing bridges. We tried to explain to him that it was totally impractical to avoid them, but he would have none of it and countered that he'd studied the map and worked out a route that would involve far fewer crossings. We just had to make our way via Dusseldorf. He lost the argument as driving an extra 500 miles was out of the question!

I don't remember much about the race, but the social scene at Zandvoort was great in those days. It is a coastal holiday resort, and as such felt much like many seaside towns in Britain such as Margate or Blackpool. But with the addition of a decidedly queer lingo, mayonnaise instead of vinegar being splattered on one's frites, and the barmen's most extraordinary habit of pouring absurdly foamy beer, then scraping the top off with a spatula. These peculiar practices caused most visiting English folk to look on aghast.

We returned to Zandvoort later in the year for an international race, with some grand prix regulars taking part - members of the famous continental circus that we were so attracted to. We wanted to see how we and our Jack Machin 125cc Yamaha measured up, but for me the big attraction was being at the seaside. We went with another rider and our future best man, Adrian Drew, who was to act as Clive's mechanic. Qualifying practice on the Saturday went well, as I remember. We were measuring up satisfactorily and looking forward to achieving a good race result the following day. In high spirits, we decided to throw ourselves at Zandvoort's funfair rides, hoopla stalls, shooting ranges, and candy floss stalls, and its bars. I did mention it was much like Blackpool, didn't I?

Well, we all got absolutely hammered. Even our erstwhile sainted rider let himself go, and it was very late when we staggered back to the race paddock to bed down for the night. Adrian crawled into his tent and Clive and I crashed out in the van. Although we were absolutely dog-tired and fell straight to sleep, we were intermittently awoken by dull thump, thump, thump sounds. It continued on and off for most of the night and in the morning I asked Adrian if he had heard it. 'It was me, I'm afraid, he said. 'I kept waking up because of the lumps in the ground. I was using the tent mallet to flatten them. Sorry if I woke you at all.'

None of us felt great that race day as we were all suffering from lack of sleep and the previous evening's over-indulgences. Our rider, usually so reliable, rode like a mincing fairy. 'I couldn't function properly,' he said. 'Nothing made sense, there was no balance, my mind was fogged.' Bloody hell, it was obvious. He shouldn't have got drunk. We all felt we had let ourselves down and missed a golden opportunity to shine. We were celebrating 24 hours too soon, well before the chequered flag was unfurled, let alone waved. Never again would we let that happen.

Neil (Tex) Tuxworth became our good friend partly as a result of a crash at his local circuit, Cadwell Park. Clive was knocked off from behind at the hairpin on the first lap of a race. The 'perp', said Clive afterwards, snarling with rage, was some fool with Tex written on his helmet. He then toured the paddock, looking for this wally but he never found him.

A couple of weeks later Neil sought us out and confessed it had been him, explaining the brake anchor his farmer friend had welded onto his bike had broken, causing loss of control and the collision. He invited us to stay in the spare caravan at his family farm any time we were at Cadwell Park in the future, an offer we accepted. A good move too, as it proved much better than sleeping in the van. We came to see that it should have come as no surprise to Neil that his brake anchor had failed. Raymond the welder's day job was milking cows, and his only metalwork qualification was that he owned an arc welding set. He couldn't see too well either, and his ancient spectacles were yellowed by nicotine and covered in spots of tobacco ash from his pipe. We got to know both Neil and his crazy friends, of which there were many, quite well. His barmpot crew acted as his mechanics, cooks and bottle washers, and they were a great bunch.

We attended each other's birthday parties and other celebrations over the years too. Neil's 21st was particularly memorable as he held it in a barn at his farm. Pete Butler, his main mechanic, staged his at the Flying Horse in Louth, and mine was at the village hall in Brailsford, Derbyshire. Everyone involved in racing seemed to turn up to these dos, no matter from how far away.

Neil has a great natural friendliness and charm, allied with an ability to manage people. Sadly Clive did not seem to learn any of Neil's diplomatic skills. I remember one day in the garage whilst preparing his bike, he let slip he would rather ride his bike than me! Not a great way to make a girl feel good about herself, is it? Especially as I'd just knitted us a pair of natty new team sweaters.

We had just been awarded sponsorship, or more accurately, given free product by the oil company, Duckhams, and I painstakingly knitted us sweaters in Duckhams blue and yellow with the letter Q (for Quality, ie: Q20/50) on the fronts as part of the pattern. That was not easy, I can tell you. The design had to be drawn out from scratch on graph paper, then translated into a pattern, then knitted. Anyway, I'd learned another skill. Who knows, I thought, I may get a job with Woman's Realm, or maybe even Cosmopolitan.

Clive was a total cretin for saying something so cruel and crude, but stick with it girls there would be worse to come! The thing is most blokes don't even feel bad for saying hurtful stuff like that. Not like I did one time at the Isle of Man TT, when, after being awoken by the alarm clock for early morning practice at 4am, I grumpily said, 'I'm not getting up at this ungodly hour. Go by yourself!' He did, too, but after he left I felt so terribly guilty I could not get back to sleep and I got up and walked two miles to the grandstand so at least I could welcome him back in. If the roles had been reversed, would that happen? We know the answer to that one don't we girls? The lazy git would've still been in bed when I got back.

I had had a bit of a sob earlier that year watching Neil on the the top step of the podium after a race at Mettet in Belgium while the British national anthem was played for him and not my bloke. Clive had had victory in the bag. He easily won the first race of a two-leg event, and he was leading by a country mile in the second. But on the final straight, on the run-in to the chequered flag and just yards from victory, the engine misfired and blew one of the exhaust pipes away from its mounting. His speed dropped dramatically and half a dozen riders flew past on the approach to the line. What cruel luck. Afterwards Neil said, 'Don't worry, you will get your luck at the TT.' A fine example of Neil's diplomacy and magnanimity, or was Mr Tuxworth a prophet?

Nevertheless, Clive and I were a team, and although it sometimes felt to me that I was the only one taking the strain and making the sacrifices, we worked together as a pair of professionals. If we had to strip carburettors, for example, he would do one, while I copied every move and took responsibility for the other. Oh yes, it wasn't all sex, drugs and rock n roll. Sometimes we got really dirty!

The 1974 Isle of Man TT

T he Isle of Man TT was a tough test for us, let me tell you. In some ways it is as mentally tough for wives, partners and mechanics as it is for the riders. At the start/finish line there was an antiquated scoreboard system operated by boy scouts that let helpers and fans in the grandstand monitor each competitor's progress around the 37¾ mile circuit. As rider X passed particular points on the track, messages confirming his position were telephoned or radioed to the scoreboard captain. Upon receipt of these, the hand on a simple clock face was manually rotated to show that rider had passed the markers at quarter-lap distance, then at the halfway point and so on. There was (still is) a long row of these clocks, one for every competitor, and below each one was a column of hooks onto which small, individually sign-written boards were hung denoting completed lap times.

Watching the boy scouts scurrying hither and thither turning those pointers (or not) is a very stressful business. Very nerve-wracking indeed. Occasionally your man appears to have crashed or retired as nothing happens for many minutes, then they turn the hand twice in one go! The system has its quirks you see. After the first three-quarters of a lap had been achieved I always felt I could relax just a little bit, as soon afterwards, with his engine screaming, Clive would flash past or whip into the pits. But then he would disappear out of sight once again, and I would return to watching the clocks and the antics of the boy scouts along with all the other nail-biting wives and girlfriends.

This was our second TT (he finished a creditable seventh on our first visit in 1973) and it started, as they all do, when we got on board the ghastly ferry from Liverpool. I remember us both leaning on the safety rail looking out to sea during the four-hour endurance test that was the crossing to Douglas in those days. The Isle of Man Steam Packet Company was a name that sounded quaintly out of date even then - something that belonged in the previous century - and its ships and the way it did business was just as old fashioned in every respect. Everything was positively Victorian, except the prices. You could cross the English Channel on roll-on-roll-off ferry in those days with four passengers in your vehicle, all for around £15, and in relative comfort. But the IOM SPCo wanted £80 and you had to sit on a slatted wooden bench. Nowadays, of course, it costs several hundred pounds to get a team across the water to Mona's Isle.

Where were we? Oh yes, leaning on the railing. We were discussing our chances of winning the 125cc event, which was why we were going, of course, although it was in the realm of dreamland. 'If I could win the TT as a privateer, I would definitely get a works ride out of it,' said Clive. A life-changing fortnight lay ahead, or so we dreamed.

We had a semi-privateer local rival called Austin Hockley. I say 'semi' as he rode for a big-hitting motorcycle dealership called Granby Motors based in Ilkeston, Derbyshire. They built and sold racing 125cc Yamaha-engined motorcycles, as well as flogging street machines for the general public, and they were very good at it too.

Austin had a team-mate, one Ivan Hodgkinson, and both their bikes were top of the range machines with water-cooled cylinders and heads that were custom-made in Holland. Very expensive indeed and well out of our price range. These special parts were fitted to the latest, bang up-to-date, Mark III Yamaha engines. Ours was a venerable Mark I, and it sported a home-made water jacket which Clive had commissioned from Steve Machin, British 125cc road racing champion and brother of Jack the frame builder. Steve hammered the cooling fins off the Yamaha's cylinders, then welded the jacket around the outside of what remained. Now this was highly skilled work, don't get me wrong, but full-on garden shed stuff all the same. Unmodified, air-cooled cylinder heads topped things off. Sadly Steve lost his life at Cadwell Park on a practice day, only a few weeks after the 1974 TT.

Our other big rival, more of a threat than Austin in fact, was a fast and stylish rider called Chas Mortimer. Chas was a former TT winner and Grand Prix regular, and he was riding a factory Yamaha. To triumph over these well-heeled fellows would be no mean feat.

During practice week friends kept coming up to me and saying how sorry they were to have found out Clive would be setting off alongside Austin. 'Oh dear,' they all said, 'you must be terribly worried.' To understand their concern I should explain that TT races were, and still are, run very differently from events on short circuits in which all the competitors are flagged off together in a screaming mob.

At the TT the riders start in pairs at ten second intervals. A TT race is therefore, in effect, a time trial and the competitor completing the course in the shortest time is the winner. More often than not the winning rider is also among the first on the road. Not always the case for sure, but true in most instances as the low numbers are always given out to experienced riders of proven ability.

At the 1974 TT Clive was given number eight, something I consider a lucky omen. All based on science, of course - I can't be doing with superstition and voodoo. Let me explain. We lived at number 26 and two and six make eight. We got married on the 19th, and nine minus one equals eight. And he finished seventh the previous year on his first visit to the TT, and seven plus one (for being first this year) is eight.

Now Austin, who was rider number seven, had a bit of a reputation for being - how can one put it delicately? - a bit mental. There, I've said it! However, being mental is a relative thing, and I am certain Austin thought he was entirely rational and of perfectly sound mind. Very few folk who knew him would agree with him on that point, but be that as it may. A magistrate, hearing someone has driven at 120mph on the motorway would consider that to be mental behaviour, but anyone involved in racing would consider it rather humdrum. It's all about perception and relativity. Still, it was rather unnerving to hear so many people express their concerns about Austin in that way.

And Austin was certainly a proper hard case. He once rode up the bank at Kate's Cottage and smashed his front wheel, damaging the hub. Did he retire? No chance, he somehow rode the bike back to the pits and wanted to continue. And he often used to be seen walking around the paddock in his leathers, hunched over, with his right hand on an invisible throttle and his left hooked over an imaginary clutch lever, just as if he was still on his bike.

I must add at this point that we always got on well with Austin. When we were racing, he always came over to me at social dos, prize givings or whatever, and dragged me onto the dance floor. He never spoke as I recall, but he did love to make wild shapes to the music with a willing partner. Skipping forward to the present for a moment, Clive and I occasionally enjoy meeting up with Austin and a bunch of other riders from days of yore to have a good natter in the pub. He is much more talkative now than he was when we were younger.

As well as the 125cc TT, we had another race to prepare for that year. Bike importers Agrati Sales, who were based in nearby Nottingham, had entered Clive, Lindsay Porter and Manx Grand Prix winner Bernard Murray in the Production TT on 250cc Benellis. We saw it as nothing more than an add-on to our main activities. A bit on the side. But hey, it meant more practice and circuit familiarisation without increased wear and tear on our little bike.

Actually, Clive absolutely loved the Benelli and it was a real shame the dratted thing never managed more than a few miles before cutting out and stopping. This occurred with tedious regularity, whereupon he would dump it at the side of the track, get a lift back to the pits, jump on the 125 and do another lap on that. Agrati's chief engineer Arthur Bullock was not from a racing background, but he was a thoroughly nice bloke and highly competent. But his name did encourage creative modification by the more roguish riders in the paddock!

I won't quote them directly here. I'll let you work it out. Yes, that's it! When practice was over and the roads reopened, 'Arfa' would despatch someone to collect the stricken Italian motorcycle and later report back each time that there was nothing wrong with it whatsoever. The same scenario played out three evenings on the trot, and we were getting heartily sick of it, and Arthur and his boys must have have been thinking Clive was an idiot. 'The mechanic rode it back,' he said on one occasion. They put a 'more mature' rider on it who completed a lap successfully, confirming perhaps that Clive was indeed the plonker they suspected he was, although they were too polite to say so. They also never said they'd found a fault, but we believe they had discovered the problem was, in fact, fuel starvation due to an insufficiently vented fuel tank, and that they were too embarrassed to confess.

Whatever. Clive rode the Benelli in the race and it absolutely flew! It handled superbly, which is why he was so fond of it, and he was soon high on the leaderboard and leading the team's other entries too! The bike never missed a beat until it reached the Waterworks on the mountain section during the final lap, whereupon, short of fuel, it spluttered and slowed. Clive kept it going after a fashion by slopping the fuel tank from side to side, using tiny throttle openings on the uphill parts, and turning the engine off and coasting down-hill. A great many riders came flying past him as he wheezed and plodded along, but he made it to the finish.

When he stopped he could hardly straighten his back as he had been lying prone over the tank for so long. He was awarded only a bronze replica for his efforts, but it is one of our more treasured trophies as it was so very hard earned.

The whole Agrati enterprise had been considered a success, nonetheless, with all three of its Benellis finishing the race. Consequently, the owner of the company took the team out for dinner at the Palace Casino, which was where all the rich folk in the Isle of Man hung out in those days. Clive and I shared a Chateaubriand for the first time (it's always a cut of meat for two - we weren't cheapskating) and we loved it. I would have been interested to see the bill at the end, but the boss was a classy guy and he discreetly took care of things.

Afterwards we went through into the gambling hall, just to look at what went off in such a swanky place. Clive decided to have a flutter on the roulette table, got a fiver out of his pocket and asked the croupier to 'give him five'. No, he wasn't after a celebratory hand smack. What he wanted was five £1 chips, but the woman thought he wanted to make a £5 bet and put our precious fiver on number five! The note disappeared into a slot and she gave it a prod with a spatula just to make sure it was utterly irretrievable. Then she spun the wheel and, of course, we lost. Clive was most upset and the speed at which the fiver had vaporised put him off gambling for life. At least when you spent a fiver on racing spares at Granby Motors, you got a bit of social intercourse thrown in, making parting with the cash a bit more more of an event in comparison.

At the Isle of Man TT, racing generally takes place in the first full week in June, with practice week preceding it. Thus the start of the festival can be on many different dates near the end of May. Once practising is over the journalists all get their portable typewriters out (laptops these days, of course), study times and form, and bang out their predictions for the races to come.

In 1974 Clive had recorded the fastest of all the 125cc practice times, but Chas was declared the probable winner and we were considered likely to finish fifth at best! I could tell Clive was incensed about this by all the snorting and fiery language. To dismiss him in such a way added fuel to his fire. His bold statement, 'I'll show the bastards,' summed up his mood and gave away the level of his intent.

There was an hour's delay due to inclement weather before the race eventually started. Chas, on the works Yamaha was one of the first two to push away, and thirty seconds later Clive and Austin were flagged off together. Our lovely blue and yellow, Duckhams-liveried bike, fired up cleanly and he was quickly underway. Austin Hockley's Granby Motors machine was somewhat reluctant to start, but it eventually chimed in and he gave chase a few seconds behind Clive. I was grateful for the gap as they plunged out of sight and down Bray Hill. By the time they reached the Crosby Straight, Austin had caught and passed Clive.

'I was wondering where he'd got to,' said Clive later. 'His bike should have been quicker than mine, so when he came by I tucked into his slipstream and followed him.'

Clive kept pace with Austin quite easily as it happened, and later decided on some mind games. 'When we approached the right hander just before the 13th milestone I thought I would pass him, just to let him know I meant business, if you see what I mean. During practice I had been testing taking one particular curve without easing the throttle. So when we arrived at this bend and Austin eased off, I shot past and promptly nearly soiled myself! The road was still wet under the trees and I remember scraping my fairing on the deck as I went into a big slide. Oops! Or words to that effect, then bless my soul, the bike popped upright again, and I was still on board, pointing in the right direction, and very much alive, albeit behind Austin, who had re-passed me during my mad moment.

'As the palpitations subsided I thought sod it, I'll follow him, it's quieter that way. I stuck to him like glue and we were almost conjoined as we approached Ramsey Square and came upon Chas on the works Yamaha. This meant Austin and I had taken 30 seconds out of him in around half a lap! Austin flashed by on one side and I shot past on the other. We were formation flying! Chas then pulled out with mysterious gear selection problems. It was for the best, I suppose. You can't have a works bike being beaten by a couple of ne'er do wells can you?'

By the time the dynamic duo reached me on the start/finish line they were still pretty well stuck together, with Clive right on Austin's tail. They soon disappeared out of sight over the Glencrutchery crossroads and it was back to watching the scoreboard. It was a worry, I will admit, but I am glad I did not witness what happened next. As they descended Bray Hill, where these ultra-lightweight bikes reach their maximum speed plunging past houses and walls and lamp posts, Clive decided he had recovered his nerve after his brush with death, and he attempted to pass Austin once again.

'I drew alongside but as we approached Ago's Leap Austin started to move across and push me towards the garden walls that line the road! Yep, the rumours were right, I concluded, he is a nutter. So once again I decided, sod it, I'll pass him later.'

Less than a minute after exiting Quarter Bridge at the bottom of the hill, Clive found a safe place to pass and Austin never troubled him again as he broke down with a basic gearbox fault, something which should never have happened to anyone in a team as good as Granby's. So when Clive came by me again he was starting the final lap, leading on the road, and leading on time as well. The margin between him and the second place man continued to grow and grow, even though he'd knocked the pace off a little to spare his engine.

I crossed all my fingers and prayed there would be no repeat of the Mettet exhaust pipe incident or any other fickle finger of fate event visited upon us from the heavens. The boy scouts turned Clive's clock hand its final few turns and soon I knew he was on the run-in to the finish. Now we only had a few more agonising minutes before the ecstasy of victory.

We waited and waited, listening for the 14,000rpm scream of our shed-built two-stroke engine. We knew we would hear the little Yamaha before we saw Clive because the finishing straight follows a gentle rise. And then he came. Nnnneeeooowwwmmm!! All yellow and blue, with a silver helmet on the top, he flashed by in a blur. Yippee, he's won! Oh my goodness, what now?

The post race palaver, that's what. The rostrum, the champagne and the press interviews. That was when Clive slipped the journalists one of his gems, describing how on the final, lonely lap, he was 'talking to his bike'. This admission wrote the headlines for the following day's sports pages. 'Talking Bike Wins the TT'. A little later, when the champagne ran dry, we, the team of two, went into Douglas for a spot of lunch. A bloke in the café asked if we knew who had won the 125cc TT that morning. 'I did,' Clive replied, matter-of-factly. 'No mate, who really won it?' 'Some geezer called Clive Horton,' said Clive. Ah well, the chap went away happy.

At the prize-giving that evening Clive received a huge trophy, engraved with famous names such as Carlo Ubbiali, Mike Hailwood, Phil Read, Chas Mortimer, Bill Ivy and a great many others besides. Freshly inscribed alongside these was now the name Clive Horton.

After a bit of a battle, it must be said, I was presented with a little trophy, for being the mechanic of the first privateer bike home. It was really important to us that we were acknowledged as a private team. And we were definitely a privateer entry. The only backing we had was free oil. But the organisers seemed reluctant to acknowledge that I was the team's mechanic. Their attitude was that they didn't normally give it to the mechanics of race winners, the glory being reward enough. In fact, they didn't normally have the conundrum at all as the winner usually wasn't a privateer or anything like it. We were totally off script!

In actual fact, and to be honest, I didn't do a great deal of spanner work on the day of that particular race. On the eve of the event our friend Pete Fawcett from Louth, one of the Tuxworth clan, gave Clive a hand, and then he was on duty in the pit box on the start line on race day. Nevertheless, I was nominally the chief mechanic, coach, team manager and 'main woman', and I was pleased to receive my little cup as a reward for my part in our success.

After another rip-off sea crossing we drove back home to Derby in our old Bedford CA van, taking the TT trophy with us in the cab. I bet that is the only time one of those magnificent old things has travelled in an old working vehicle like that. We gave Derby-based journalist Chris Carter a lift home, which didn't leave a lot of space! (He was, and is, a big chap). He carried the trophy on his lap. Chris was a track commentator and he worked for Motorcycle Weekly, ghosting Chas Mortimer's regular column and editing his own 'Paddock Gossip' page as well as writing race reports. He always had time to chat as that's how he got a lot of his information, and he is a real people person. If he spotted me walking through the paddock, he'd stop me and ask me how Clive was getting on. Clever really. At the Dutch TT at Assen one year it was the day of Clive's birthday. I mentioned it to Chris and he said: 'Ooh, I must write that down and use it in my commentary this afternoon.'

Back to the 1974 TT and I have to add a dash of pathos. Remember our day-dream on the outgoing ferry? The belief that success would open the doors of opportunity? Clive told me that as he crossed the line and passed the chequered flag he said to himself, 'It's not enough. It is just not enough... Oh bugger! How disappointing. Never mind, let's just enjoy the moment, the back-slapping and champagne for what it is worth, and see where life goes...'

These thoughts were processed on the short ride back to the pits (One doesn't do a lap of honour at the TT, you just stop after the chequered flag and double back to the park ferme on a service road), but he did a professional job when he spoke to the press. You would never have known he'd just experienced this emotional cocktail of euphoria and sadness.

This 'not enough' thinking was not about dissatisfaction with winning. He had won a TT. What more can one do? It was more the realisation it was not good enough just to win. He wanted to show the world how marvellous he was by winning in a spectacular, and swashbuckling manner; riding to glory with all the style and panache of Errol Flynn. But on the day it just didn't happen that way.

You have to bear in mind it had been seven whole years since Bill Ivy had taken the ultra-lightweight class TT lap record to over 100mph. Little Bill had done this on an exotic four-cylinder factory Yamaha churning out more than 40bhp. Since then the rules had been changed and such creations had been outlawed. There was not a hope in hell that the twin-cylindered, essentially road bike-engined, home-modified bikes of 1974 would even get close to Bill's times. They made little more than half the power.

Clive was disappointed that his main opposition was not up to pushing him harder, and he is still a little glum about it to this day. How sad is that? Good grief, he won a TT. He rode brilliantly. Enough, already!

Married at last

W hat happened next? Well, in my capacity as main sponsor, team manager, chief critic and life coach, I thought I would put my foot down with a firm hand (!). He can jolly well marry me or buy his own van! He couldn't afford a new van so there was nothing to discuss. We got married in the October of that year.

The wedding reception was a fairly low key affair at the local pub. Dad had given us the choice of a few quid towards setting up house and home, or enough for a big wedding. We chose the sensible option, of course. With that money, we bought all the domestic stuff newlyweds need. Habitat, G-Plan and some bits from an arty shop in Matlock. Dad's attitude to Clive had mellowed hugely by now, after five rollercoaster racing years, and I had been patient throughout this time waiting for a proposal that never came. In the end it was time to issue an ultimatum. I guess conventional behaviour from an unconventional bloke, was always too much to hope for.

The wedding went well, amazingly! A bit of bullying from Adrian, the best man, to get the groom to wear a tie was the only sticky moment. The local paper turned up to take the star's (not me - him!) wedding pictures, although people did say I looked stunning in my wide-brimmed hat.

Dad's speech was a highlight for me, and very much the icing on the wedding cake when he referred to us as 'proving to be quite a team' and said our 'marriage would be team enterprise' and all that jazz. So far, forty odd years later, he's been on the money. The honeymoon started the following day in the paddock at Snetterton. Yep, we went racing!

We put an advertisement 'TT-winning Team Looking For Sponsor' in Motorcycle News, and luckily it was answered by a used car dealer called Robin Mayne. Robin was a self-made man, as the cliche goes, about a decade our senior. Married to Maureen with two young daughters, he had moved from London to Nantwich in Cheshire and made an absolute fortune buying and selling second-hand cars. We arranged to meet up at the Greyhound pub in Findern near Derby as he used to visit his Mum nearby every couple of weeks. Isn't it strange how sometimes things just fall into place and obviously were just meant to be, and other times everything's such an uphill struggle it might be better not to have bothered.

Anyway, we really hit it off with Robin and we all had some great adventures together over the next few years. None were really planned, but that is one of the best things about adventures. Things should come as a surprise.

Robin bought us a Yamaha TZ250 from John Cooper, who did a bit of 'grey importing' of race bikes and spare parts as a sideline to his garage work. We got a bit of a discount as the bike was slightly damaged after having been dropped from a crane while being unloaded at dockside. It wasn't too badly beaten up, but nevertheless Rob got a deal and car traders love a deal!

He also fixed us up with a white Transit van, as by now the Qualcast Bedford had run its last race. We sold it for £25. It had been a loyal servant and it was a sad day. But to heck with sentimentality, we were ready for a bit more speed and a comfort upgrade.

The green Bedford had been requiring more and more effort to keep it on the road. At one stage it developed a rather noisy back axle and the lads at the garage where I worked diagnosed a duff diff. Clive and I raked around in a local scrapyard, finally finding a similar model to ours from which we extracted a replacement axle. One of the less romantic Sunday afternoons I have spent!

The 1975 season started with Clive winning the East Midlands ACU 250cc Championship. Let me explain - it was just one race at Cadwell Park. The new bike was actually not all that fast, but Clive managed to snatch the lead by adopting an aggressive move on the final bend. We put the machine's lack of performance down to newness, and its unfamiliarity to the rider.

We carried on racing both the 125 and the 250 at the same meetings wherever we could, in both club and national championship events. The 250cc results were not as good as we had expected and we were clueless as to why? Maybe the rider was rubbish? Heaven forbid!

We went to the 1975 TT and did all the practice sessions, both the early morning ones held at the crack of dawn, and the teatime outings in the early evening. Being June though, it very often meant these were the finest times of the day, weather-wise, although it did mean that low-lying sun sometimes blinded the riders.

The lap times were not all that marvellous to be honest, Clive described the bike as 'uninspired', and when a bike is mediocre it infects the rider. This works both ways, actually. If the bike feels up for it and raring to go, the rider usually feels enthused.

After final practice, in a desperate attempt to conjure up some more speed, we changed the only piece of 'black magic' on the bike. It was a big decision, too. A new ignition system was three weeks' wages at the time. Expensive voodoo.

When the bike was restarted, it made us jump out of our skins. It sounded angry, mean, crisp and ready for action. Chuffed would not adequately describe our newly positive mindset. Practice was all over, so the system couldn't be tested and some settings had to be guessed at. We just hoped for the best.

For the race, Robin decided he would be Clive's pit crew for the scheduled refuelling stop. Shock was the look on Robin's face as his rider approached him head-on in the pit box with the front wheel locked and the back one hovering in the air. Robin dived over the pit wall, then scrambled back as Clive paddled the bike backwards a couple of yards. 'My whole life passed before my eyes,' was Robin's comment after the refuelling was done. He didn't blink for several minutes.

I sat in the grandstand watching all this unfold, thinking Robin will need a stiff drink at the end of this race. Robin and his pal David Williams had some good late night sessions with me. That pair could take a drink or two. The rider was usually tucked up in bed! Checking the records, I see Clive finished eighth in that race - that lucky number once again.

After the TT, we went with David to race in the 125cc and 250cc classes at the Belgian Grand Prix. I guess Robin had to work that week. We travelled overnight and reached the city of Liege around 6am. It was a seminal moment for us as we sat in a streetside cafe adjacent to the railway station, taking an early morning coffee and watching a continental city come to life.

Seeing all those poor wretches dashing to work, made us realise we were privileged to be out of the rat race, at least for a while. Man, we were feeling happy and relaxed. Some distance away we could see in the early morning mist a large, rather imposing church on a hilltop. We decided to walk up to it and have a look. History and geography are never far away. It turned out to be a cathedral with lumps bitten out of the masonry and bullets chips here and there, all presumably from it seeing action in the Second World War.

Clive and I were quite shy, but David just opened the heavy church door and walked right in. We followed. The cathedral had obviously been unlocked all night. What trust! I wonder if they lock it these days, after forty or more years of declining human standards? Wow! It was an utterly impressive building with a cupola roof and the acoustics were just a marvel. The preacher's dais had a microphone and one could easily imagine hellfire and damnation ringing in the congregation's ears during Sunday mass. I'm sure anyone would be a quaking believer after that.

They call the Assen circuit in Holland the cathedral of motorcycling, but the Belgian Grand Prix's traditional home at Spa Francorchamps was a wonderful bike racing circuit too. But the paddock? What a total dump. Half the motorcycling world would attend that race and all those miserable sods the owners could supply for the teams was a filthy toilet you had to pay to use and cold showers. Even those, it was rumoured, used recycled water!

The weather was absolutely perfect which is most unusual for the Ardennes. It invariably rains there, but in 1975 we never saw a drop. Sadly, I had no sun gear with me, so I just wandered about in my underwear. Some of the paddock seemed quite pleased to see me, and when I turned up on the pit wall to lap score I did feel quite brave. Others, perhaps, thought I was a tad brazen. Whatever, it's nice to engender a smile or two.

Before practice began, when things were still all quiet and relaxed, Clive and I had a walk around the paddock, just to check everything out. This is where we first got to know Irishman Tom Herron and his English wife Andrea. We had much in common. Both couples were recently married and both riders were battling to establish themselves in the teeth of tough competition.

They were further along the road than we were, of course, and had been part of the continental circus for a couple of years. Living hand to mouth in a truck and caravan, Tom and Clive had shared the rostrum at the TT only twelve months previously, Tom finished third in the race Clive won, so we felt a kind of rapport. We were however, about to receive a lesson.

As a conversation opener, Clive said, 'Hi Tom, how are you doing?' The response was as you get from anyone in these situations, cliched and noncommittal. In an effort at deeper engagement, Clive asked if Tom knew the gearing here at Spa. This is a fairly innocuous question to pose at a regular race venue, and a way to encourage a general chat about other matters.

Not at this professional level, it appeared. Not when you are racing for prize money and world championship points. At a Grand Prix no quarter should be asked for, or given. It was a gladiatorial arena, and Tom's response was a sharp retort. 'Mallory Park!' he said, which was clearly absurd as no circuit could be less like that tight little Leicestershire former trotting track than the fast, sweeping forested expanses of Spa Francorchamps. Furthermore, the reply was spat out with such venom it made us step back slightly and halted all our efforts at friendliness. Yes, he was rude, but it was a great lesson to learn and Tom was often thanked subconsciously for it, if not directly in person.

I can't remember the outcome of the races, but the 250cc bike developed a rear puncture while Clive was battling with Mick Grant on his works Kawasaki. Mind you, that was before that particular green meanie became the all-conquering world championship-winning machine exploited by Kork Ballington and Toni Mang.

The following year I gave birth to our first son, Daniel. He was born one month prematurely, probably due to the fact Clive had me helping to push-start his bike at Snetterton the week before. I was still in maternity when Clive and Robin decided they would go to Mettet in Belgium, to race the next weekend. So when I tell you racing blokes are awfully selfish people, you can see I have experienced it first hand, and it's not in any way made up!

My baby boy had jaundice, but I wanted to be out of hospital when Clive and Robin returned so, following doctor's orders, I walloped water down that baby's throat at every opportunity and we made it. The Belgian meeting was not so hot, results wise, but Clive had very much mixed it with some of the Grand Prix stars of the day, people like Kork Ballington, Penti Korhonen and Chas Mortimer, until he broke down with a seized main bearing. I didn't like to miss the annual trip to Mettet as it was always such a fun meeting, and I vowed not to be left behind again.

When Daniel was only a few weeks old we three, along with with Robin and David, went to the Paul Ricard circuit in the south of France, to take part in the Moto Journal 200, a meeting in which a 250cc race took place alongside the big name 750cc event. Paul Ricard is a very long way indeed, especially in a Transit van carrying four adults and a baby, but we never once fell out, even when Clive took over the driving on the Paris Peripherique late at night and got us hopelessly lost.

We all fell asleep and left him to it. He knew we just had to keep heading south, so what could be simpler? Well, the way he tells it he knew we were aiming next for a city that had a name beginning with L, so when he started seeing signs for Lille, he went for it!

An hour or so later he was feeling rather tired, so he pulled over into a service area to change drivers and get some shut-eye. By now Paris was well and truly behind us. We were well on our way and it was someone else's turn. Having pulled up and visited the gents, he spent a few minutes studying the road map which these places often have handily framed and fastened to a wall. Scratching his head, he called us over and said he couldn't find where we were.

He was looking south of Paris, of course, and that was the problem. Once we looked north of Paris, on the way to Lille, in fact, it dawned on him that we had been travelling in entirely the wrong direction for quite some time, and Lyon, the city that was next on our route, was now an extra 120km away from us. Oh calamity!!

We all remained calm. You have to expect set-backs when you are travelling with a wally, it's only to be expected. 'Well Lille does begin with an L.' he pleaded. Fortified by strong coffee we set off southward once again, and Paris, Lyon, Mt Ventoux, Avignon, Nimes and many other romantic names whizzed by en route to Paul Ricard.

When we arrived the following afternoon the notorious mistral wind was blowing with monstrous force. What Beaufort number it was I know not, but it was impossible to pitch the tent. Oh, have I mentioned this extra bonus that goes with knocking about with a motorcycle racer? The exciting camping trips!

By this time we had upgraded our canvas accommodation and bought a big frame tent with an annexe which we used as a workshop. That night, though, all five of us had to sleep in the van. Robin's nerves were getting a little frayed by now, but his pal David kept him from losing his cool and flying back home. Overnight the mistral ran out of puff and became a zephyr, and in the morning the tent was hurriedly pitched, although not without difficulty. It's not easy banging crappy monkey metal tent pegs into rock-hard mediterranean terrain.

Nonetheless we managed it, but as the day drew on and practice started the mistral got its breath back and blew mightily down the long back straight. The bikes absolutely flew with its assistance. Robin's mood was picking up, too, especially as Clive was the only Brit to qualify. There was nothing scheduled for the following day, so we all went into the nearest town for the evening. Bandol is a delightful French port, with a harbour full of modest watercraft, rather like that of a Cornish fishing village, but a bit posher. Definitely worth a visit any time you are down that way.

Our object was to celebrate David's 32nd birthday, a particularly auspicious one for him as his own father died before reaching that age. We found a restaurant, put the baby to bed in his carrycot in the van, and went and had a great meal. The food was wonderful and we got soundly pissed. When you look back it was all so reckless. Although we were constantly checking on the baby, nowadays we read about parents being hauled into court for doing that sort of thing and we would have absolutely no sympathy. Hang the wretches, or tie them to a grating and flog them at the very least!

Well, we were not done yet. In our party-going state we befriended the local postman and his pals, who invited us all back to his place for some sort of potent and illicit drink called 'essence of wine'. It was made from grape seeds, stalks and skins, if I remember correctly. Anyway it was paint stripper. So we drank it!

Things got out of hand when one of the Frenchies made a pass at me, whereupon at long last Clive called the stupidity to a halt. The only problem was we were all virtually paralytic, in charge of a small baby, and we had to drive the van up a precipitous mountain track to return to the circuit. As the least smashed out of his mind, David was given the keys while Clive and I went to the back of the van and laid down on our bellies. Then, with the back doors wide open, we vomited again and again as we wound our way up the mountain.

Robin meanwhile was shouting 'Hughey McGrew' out of the passenger window. We should all have been jailed!

The following morning there was further bedlam in the camp. Clive was chucking stuff about, shouting that his trainers had been stolen in the night. They were later found in his tool box. Now how did that happen? Robin, who had been sleeping on the front seats of the van, was also panicking. He was desperate for a wee and he could not find his penis. The poor bloke had put his long johns on backwards. How did that happen? Dave was just happy to be older than his dad, and baby Daniel, asleep in his cot, was none the wiser, thank goodness.

The shape of things to come. The Brader's Maico

A big test we didn't need

O n race weekends back home in the UK we developed a successful, if exhausting routine. Very early on Saturday mornings I would pick Clive up in a van loaded with bikes, tools, baby and food after he had worked the Friday night shift at the foundry where he was now a supervisor. I would then drive to the race track whilst he slept. He would then win, then I would drive us all home again. Occasionally we were both so absolutely knackered we had to pull over and sleep in a lay-by, on our way home.

Once, around midnight, we were shocked awake by banging on the side of the van. It was a prying policeman demanding to know what we were up to. We explained and, disbelieving, he smirked most annoyingly. He needed a punch in the face, but didn't get one. He then insisted he was concerned for our safety and we should move the van over the road and park it in a field. We were so dog tired we did as we were told. He may not have been a dirty voyeur, but that is how he is remembered.

It was during this period we began a superstitious ritual which stemmed from a moment of panic on the grid. The bike had sprung a water leak, so I dashed back to the van, broke an egg into a jug, whisked it up with some water, and raced back to the start line where I poured the sticky mixture into the radiator.

It did the trick very well. The leak was sealed and Clive won the race, and from then on, for some time afterwards, we repeated the lucky procedure on the start line at every event. It must have worked, as he kept on winning! Of course, it was not long before people were suspecting us of putting something special and no doubt illegal into the radiator on the start line, something which gave Clive more speed and an unfair advantage. Yep! That's right guys. It was a poached egg!

Others wanted to measure the engine on the 250cc bike. Of course, being suspected of cheating is the very highest compliment you can ever be paid as a racer. It means your competitors are uncomprehending of your talents. Talents that have taken five years, much work, sacrifice and a TT win to hone, so I should flaming well think so. It was around this time that one of the Brader brothers introduced himself. The Braders, Brian and David, were a pair of mad-keen motorcycle racing enthusiasts from Grantham with very tolerant wives! They were just regular family guys with ordinary jobs but by clubbing together, they had managed to buy a super, West German, Maico machine and they wanted to see it win races. They thought Clive was a super rider and they decided he was the man to ride their treasured motorbike.

It turned out to be great bit of sponsorship for us. The brothers prepared the bike and we just turned up, and Clive generally won. Except on one day, when, after he had won an event on Robin's 250, the Braders decided to celebrate with us by opening a bottle of champagne. We all had a glass or two, even Clive, who then went out on the Maico and promptly crashed it while miles in the lead. So listen up everybody, let's be careful out there. Don't drink and drive - it turns you into an eejit. But on the whole we had a great time on that Maico. At the first ever British Grand Prix at Silverstone (after the TT lost its world championship status), Clive passed riders right and left on every fast corner, only to be overtaken by the very fast Morbidellis on the long straights. This pattern repeated itself lap after lap. It was an absolute thrill to watch and the crowd loved it, but it must have been even more fun to be doing it.

The Dutch TT also made it onto to our calendar in that fabulous, long hot summer of 1976, which everyone of a certain age remembers fondly and continues to hope something similar will happen again before we all curl our toes up. It was as hot as hell in Holland. Not something that the Dutch TT is known for. It usually rains. On the first morning, while I was busy getting together some breakfast, I could not take my eyes off one of the Brader children who was accompanying his Dad for the weekend. He was a round, chunky sort of boy and no wonder! This lad ate a bowl of casserole dish proportions, full to overflowing with Sugar Puffs. And when he'd finished, his dad gave him a second helping! Did Brader Junior become a champion darts player I wonder?

Actually, we came across this fellow again about 30 years later at a race school we were involved with at Donington Park. No longer a record-breaking devourer of vast volumes of Sugar Puffs, he was now a mature motorcyclist, teacher and a CNC machine programmer. It was great to catch up with him again and to hear about his life since that weekend in the Netherlands. He had not had an altogether easy time, and some of his story was difficult to listen to.

Back to the Dutch TT, 1976. When practising was done for the day and the track fell quiet, Clive suggested to his younger brother, David - 12-years-old at the time - that he should take a walk round the circuit. The original Assen track was about four miles long, but off he went! Even more amazingly he went all the way round without short-cuts, returning in a state of near exhaustion. What a horrible big brother David had. 'Ah, it's all part of ze training,' said Clive. Rather surprisingly, young David did not end up running away and joining the French Foreign Legion.

The Maico broke a gear lever during the race. Drat! While he sat out the rest of the race in boiling sunshine, one of the marshals offered

Clive a cool drink from his flask. Clive reckoned it was pure nectar, the best thing he'd ever tasted. It was actually ice cold Chocco Melk, a continental delight Clive is no longer allowed to enjoy, as he's now a diabetic.

In 1975 Clive and Neil Tuxworth had shared a bike once again, this time in the 1975 Production TT. It was a Honda 400/4 and they finished third in the 500cc class. In 1976 they teamed up once more and entered the same event on a tuned, bored-out version of the same bike. 'Nasty' was the way Clive described it. It also afforded me another, much worse, TT scoreboard experience, watching the boy scouts moving clock dials and hanging sign-written lap times from my position in the pit lane. Or rather this time I watched them updating other people's information, but not Clive's. Not moving the dial, not moving the dial, not moving the dial. Not… moving… the… dial. The commentators who had been rabbiting on about the leaders stopped mentioning him some time before, but without explanation, and still… the hand… did… not… move. And time, like the clock hand, stood still.

Then I saw two men walking purposefully towards me down the pit lane. I remember they were wearing black, I knew it was me they were heading for and sure enough: 'Is your rider number such and such?' I nodded. 'He's unconscious and he's been airlifted to Noble's hospital.' I had been expecting this for a while, or worse. Ever since the dial had stopped moving and the commentators moved the story on without him playing his part, but that's no help. It was a horrid feeling.

Neil tried to ease my fears. 'Not to worry, it's not a fast part of the course.' Thanks Neil, but it didn't help much. He wasn't taking into account that in 1973 I was with them in the vehicle, when he drove Clive round showing him the ropes, and that I'd driven a great many laps myself since then. I knew the section quite well.

51

Our team had a no turn off rule. If we used the circuit during open road periods, we had to continue all the way round. It was no good just doing a couple of miles, doing what we needed to do, and then turning around or cutting back the short way. Oh no, we had to finish the lap off, do the full 37.75 miles. It was as if we were scared of upsetting the giro or erasing track knowledge. Success at the TT is 90 percent about circuit knowledge and ten percent balls and ability. I just had to get down to Noble's Hospital and find out how Clive was for myself. Now then, when you arrive and find your man has regained consciousness it's a great and wonderful relief. Or is it? I'll tell you this, when he dishes out a good bollocking, saying: 'What you doin' 'ere? I've only got a couple of broken toes,' it is difficult not to smite him mightily with the ward fire extinguisher!

He was utterly battered, though, and he had a bit of red raw road rash, the scars of which are still visible today. In fact, some road tar penetrated his flesh and the skin then healed over it. No big deal, it doesn't give him any gip. He was always a lucky b*****d.

Looking back through the events of that day I could almost have predicted the outcome. Baby Daniel had a bad night, so we had had little sleep. Bleary-eyed, Clive had to get up extra early to ride the bike to pre-race technical control or scrutineering, as it was called. Our mechanics had refused to ride the bike they hated it so much. You can't blame them.

During that pre-dawn ride, through the narrow, steep streets of Douglas, Clive lost balance and toppled off when the forks hit the steering stops on a tight, downhill hairpin bend. The only damage was torn fuel lines, but it meant he had to make a hurried repair back in the workshop, before setting off to the scrutineering bay once again.

Upon arrival he handed Mr Nasty over to Neil's mates from the Lincolnshire mafia and cadged a lift back to our digs. The guest house where we were staying was a large Victorian building, run by an old grumpy couple. Stereotypical boarding house proprietors who had no doubt undergone their training across the water in Blackpool. Picture Rigsby from Rising Damp!

It was cheap, though. All the team stayed there, including Neil's mum and dad and Clive's parents, Reg and Ivy. Reg said one day he saw the proprietor stoking a very smoky yard fire. 'I think he was burning miscarriages,' he said. Yuk, but it does help draw a mental picture of this seedy guest house.

It was Neil's job to take care of the start and the first two laps of the ten lap marathon, and at breakfast Neil asked Clive if he was coming up to the start line to see him off. Clive jokingly replied: 'No, I'll have a shower. I don't want to go to hospital dirty.' Prophetic humour?

Neil made a fine start and immediately went into the lead. He held onto it for his two laps, but over the mountain section Roger 'Sooty' Sutcliffe was flying and reeling Neil in hand over fist, and Clive started his stint with the knowledge that Sooty was now 'right up our pipe.' Off he went, riding like blazes, but he overdid it and crashed on the right hander going into Kirk Michael village.

Ironically, Sutcliffe had broken down a couple of minutes before the changeover, so at the time of the crash we were miles in the lead and under no pressure at all. There had been no need for flat out antics. Clive described the incident thus. "The visor tear-off kept buzzing in my ear when I sat up out of the wind and it was incredibly irritating. The last thing I remember about going into Kirk Michael that day, was the effing buzzing! Then it all went black.' Tear-offs are clear plastic strips which fit over the visor in layers. These can be torn off and thrown away one at a time when the rider's vision gets overly restricted by dead fly spatter (or the fried egg splat of a single bumble bee or a big bug hit at high speed). The strips have an extension on one end which the rider can grasp quickly between gloved thumb and forefinger.

Clive was knocked unconscious although he does recall momentarily coming to while lying on the pavement and saying to the medic staring down at him, 'Just give me a minute to get my breath back and I'll be on my way.' The medic said; 'You are going nowhere my lad. The helicopter is on its way.' Then Clive slipped back into unconsciousness and he has no recollection of his helicopter trip. Many years later we stood spectating at the same corner and someone said: 'Hey, you're Clive Horton aren't you? We all thought you were dead when you crashed here you know. As you lay there one of your legs went into spasm and then it went still. Oooh, it was 'orrible.'

Damn and blast it! The chance of another TT win was lost, whether for want of accurate information about his rival's misfortune, or because of parental exhaustion, who knows? If we could have wound the clock back things could have been oh so different. Ah yes, but I guess everyone's life is crammed with ifs, buts and maybes. Here's another thing. On Horton race outings, in any moment of crisis I was expressly forbidden from showing emotion or shedding tears. 'It does not help the situation,' said Clive. He may well have been right, but he's still a b*****d!

The ten lap production TT had taken place on the first day after practice week, and Clive was released from Nobles Hospital the following day, which was a Sunday. He hobbled out on crutches and very much the worse for wear, with just five days to recover before the 250cc Junior race on the following Friday morning.

He went to see the stewards of the meeting, to tell them he felt able to ride Robin's Mayne Line Yamaha, as we called it, but they said he would need to show them a certificate of fitness from a designated doctor. 'Just a tip, lad. A bit of advice,' one of them said. 'Don't go in to see the doc on your crutches.'

Later, when he came out of the doctor's office walking gingerly, and a little unsteadily, but smiling, I knew he had been passed fit. But he so bloody obviously was not fit, it was ridiculous. I thought the system stank!

As it happened the race was postponed by one day due to bad weather and as we were booked on a ferry, and changing the arrangements would be a huge headache, we took all this as sign and withdrew from the event. Abba's Fernando and Cliff's Devil Woman accompanied us on the radio as we trundled home and the Worzels were number one with Combine Harvester. Oo arr! Can you believe that?

Clive finished the season as 1976 British 125cc Champion, but it hardly seemed worthwhile, becoming a national champion in those days. Nobody was really bothered or took the titles seriously. Our race federation didn't that's for sure, and the Auto Cycle Union were the promoters of the series. All you received for your efforts back then was a poxy star-shaped silver lapel badge about half an inch in diameter.

A new idea

T he 1977 season saw us competing in a dynamic new one-make series. The idea behind the Honda 125cc Championship was that all the riders would be evenly matched on low cost machines. Every bike would be technically identical, and completely unmodified in any way shape or form. This rule would be strictly monitored and enforced by official Honda scrutineers.

Each machine was owned and entered by a different Honda retailer and we were lucky to get on board with a chap called Ken Foster, a director of Fosters of Chorleton, a dealership near Manchester. Ken said his best mechanic would prepare the bike for us, and he would pay all the running costs and transport it to the events. We could keep all the prize money. That was an unexpected bonus as most sponsors liked to have a share of the spoils. Ken was a treasure.

The no-modifications, no-tuning rules were rigorously enforced from the very first event, much to everyone's surprise. Most riders are cynical about this sort of thing, but when one guy turned up with his front brake disc drilled to reduce weight and improve cooling, a fairly innocuous if rather obvious modification, he was given short shrift. After scrutineering, where the machines are checked for safety and compliance with the regulations, he was sent home and not allowed back into the championship for the rest of the season!

This strict adherence to the rules and extremely stern punishment got everyone's attention big time. And it pleased Clive hugely because it made his life easier. He is too naive to cheat, preferring to ride harder, and this championship was playing to his strengths. That year we were also riding the Brader brothers' Maico, Robin's

TZ250, and a 350cc MV Agusta twin which we took to the TT. What an expedition that turned out to be!

His lordship was racing the 125 Honda on the mainland on the very day the ferry left, which left yours truly to act as team roadie, taking care of arrangements and a van loaded with bikes, a toddler, and our huge frame tent complete with workshop annexe. Oh yes, he was still showing me a good time! It was a big ask, but all part of the job as a racer's wife. They expect much of us, but we are a resourceful breed and rarely fail.

With my faithful aide de camp, my now 13-year-old brother-in-law David, I had to drive to Liverpool to get to the then horrible Albert Dock near the Liver building, and wait in an enormous queue that stretched as far as the eye could see. You never knew if, or when, you'd actually get on a ferry. Still, it gave me time to feed Daniel with one of his favourite delicacies: the flask of baked beans I'd prepared earlier.

What a palaver. A spoonful of beans would be halfway down Daniel's throat when some jobsworth stevedore would want me to move forward a few yards. This went on for ages, until, it was finally my turn to squeeze the van through a tiny door in the side of the ship and jiggle it into position for the voyage. It wasn't a massive roll-on-roll-off thing like we have nowadays. Oh no, this was the equivalent of an indoor arena trials section, where you go on and on, inching round impossibly tight turns. It was like a helter-skelter, with no room for error, and each team vehicle in turn went jiggling, juggling, backing and forwarding until we find ourselves stuffed in together, perched on a ridiculous slope somewhere deep in the bowels of the vessel.

And as I staggered out in the gloom, baby under one arm, associated accoutrements in the other, sweary scousers were to be seen roping motorbikes to the deck and to each other, and then, as I reached the upper reaches and saw a chink of daylight, I recall thinking, Oh my God, it looks like a storm is brewing.

Clive preparing to become 1977 Honda Champion. I was pregnant with our daughter Emma

The four-hour crossing turned out to be uneventful, thank goodness. However, when we reached Douglas it was low tide, which meant the easily negotiated (in retrospect) level gang-plank we had driven across at the Albert dock was not an option here. I had to get the van up a slippery metal ramp angled at something like 45 degrees. Where is that idiot husband of mine whenever I really need him?

Following a great deal of encouragement from the Steam Packet stevedores, I hit the gas and dumped the clutch, and we shot out of that ship like a cannon ball, landing safely on the dockside. Who needs men anyway?

Our next destination was the 'paddock hotel', as it was christened - by those who shunned bricks and mortar accommodation in Douglas - for a fortnight under canvas. I would have much preferred a real hotel if I'm honest, but we were fed up with grubby guest houses and we couldn't afford a fortnight in a decent hostelry.

I erected our tent, keeping a keen eye on Daniel, now a toddler and up to mischief as little boys usually are. I was due to meet Clive off the ferry the following day but as I busied myself setting up camp the sod appeared at the tent entrance. He'd only flown over after crashing the Honda, so it had all been a pointless exercise and an unnecessary trauma. Certainly, a part of the racer's wife exam I would have preferred not to have sat.

I don't remember much about the races that year, The little MV Agusta broke its primary chain during the first lap. It was a poor motorbike really despite its exotic name, and technically more than 25 years out of date. It was probably the only machine being raced that week that still used a chain to drive its gearbox. It sounded fine, though, and it had the magic MV Agusta badge on the tank. Sadly, this didn't compensate for it being utter crap.

Back on the mainland, the Honda series was proving a mighty tussle all year with several different riders capable of mixing it at the front. This was not surprising really, considering the prize money on offer at each round. There was a three hundred quid cheque for a win, and another hundred was paid out by Champion Spark Plugs to whoever recorded the fastest lap of the race. The series attracted a few stars from the big capacity classes, but they didn't have an easy time of it from Clive and the other small bike specialists. I think the required work rate during the races, which were often hectic to say the least, was more than some of them could manage.

There is nothing like good prize money to grab a rider's attention, particularly my bloke, and he set about winning the series overall. Indeed, when the final round came around at Brands Hatch there was only one other competitor with a realistic chance of beating Clive to the title. So when Derek Huxley crashed on the second corner of the race all we had to do was finish better than sixth. So that's where he sat for a couple of steady laps, until all hell suddenly broke loose! His times dropped and he started going like the clappers. What is he doing? I thought. There is no need for this. My nerves were shredding,

At this time I was pregnant with our second child and the £1,000 award for winning the series would come in very handy indeed. All he had to do was cruise home and it was in the bag. What was going on? He was so much quicker than anyone else out on track it looked like the fastest lap money was coming our way, but he was being reckless in my view. Clive finished second behind Bernard Murray, taking the title and setting a new lap record in the process.

Later Clive explained he had been bored 'dolloping' around (a racer's term for riding unreasonably slowly), so he thought he'd try and catch the race leader 'just for a bit of fun', as Bernard had been miles in front at that point. He finished, as he put it, 'right up Bernard's pipe'. Phew, thank goodness that was over. I did get my first ride in a winner's car that day, cruising around the circuit with Clive while he waved to the fans. It was a nice bit of compensation for him causing me so much unnecessary grief.

Joining the circus

Front page of the Grantham News? We were aiming for much more

The following season saw us making our way as a professional team, racing for a living without a 'day job' to help pay the bills. Gone was the comparative safety of Clive's regular foundry supervisor work which had been bringing in over £100 per week! When you consider our mortgage was only £10 a week at that time, you can see that if it were not for racing we would have been comfortably off. Yet here we were, despite having a second child on the way, jeopardising everything by joining the 'continental circus'. Reckless? Yes, to a degree, but you only get one go at life so get out there and live it!

We had a new companion in the team for 1978, a wonderful engineer called Trevor Smedley, who would act as our chief mechanic. Trevor had been a friend for a year or so, having previously spannered for another racer, our good friend Leigh Notman. Readers paying full attention will have noted that we'd known Leigh since our earliest days in the mad and wonderful sport that is motorcycle racing.

The Braders supplied a 125cc MBA and good ol' dependable Robin once again came up with new 250cc and 350cc TZ Yamahas. A firm called Wide Range Engineering provided us with a long-wheelbase diesel Transit van. We had our own caravan, an Eldiss Sirocco fitted with an awning which we used as a semi al fresco workshop. Who was Al Fresco by the way? The guy who invented outdoor eating!

Whatever, we'd moved on from tents at last. Yippee! And what's more as head of catering, I would have four burners, a grill and a sizeable oven. I still dreamed of having a fridge.

But I'm getting ahead of myself a little bit. Before we could hit the trail and continue our adventures, I had to deliver our second child, Emma. Had we done the Beckham thing, we would have called her Douglas or Paddock, but that would have been a bit much for the poor girl, so we named her Emma, like quite a few other girls of that era. Whoever came up with the Avengers character Emma Peel has a lot to answer for.

Clive had given in his notice at the foundry and was working his final shift, Trevor was working on the bikes in the garage, and I had gone down to the bank to get some Dutch currency ready for our first race meeting of the year in Holland, when I had an almighty twinge. Emma was about to emerge, no doubt about it.

After gathering the guilders I calmly 'warm-footed' it back home. I was reluctant to 'hot-foot' it as there was no need to over-react, but we needed to get a bit of a move on, nonetheless. Once home, I telephoned Clive at work and asked him to leave early and take me to hospital.

'Don't panic, Mr Mainwaring,' was his response. 'I'll be home pronto.' But two hours later… still no sign of him! Trevor, a calm individual in almost any circumstances, was getting a bit hot under the collar. Frightened, I think, that he may have had to add midwifery, to his list of toolmaking and engineering qualifications, he eventually rang the foundry back and told Clive to '…get home bloody sharpish. This woman is about to give birth'.

'I won't be long,' was the response. 'I'll come as soon as I've run off these last two tons of molten steel.' Trevor twitched slightly, then bellowed into the receiver: 'Forget-the-f****ng-molten-steel-and-get-your-bloody-arse-home!' Finally realising the seriousness of the situation, Clive pedalled home frantically on his pushbike, arriving seriously out of breath. We then clambered into the Transit and sped to the hospital.

So just as had been the case when Daniel arrived, I was stuck in hospital with a new-born baby when Clive and Trevor went off to the season opener at Hengelo in Holland. Damn and blast it, I missed out again! I did not see him win the 125cc race, or have a super ride on the 250 at a very wet meeting where, coincidentally, the lovely Joanna Lumley, the actress who played Purdy in the New Avengers - replacing the Emma Peel character in the original series - presented the prizes. I heard about it all when they returned and handed over the prize money for me to take to the bank.

My first outing of 1978 was our trip down to the Moto Journal event at Paul Ricard. The caravan was loaded to the gunwales with hundreds of those miniature jars of Cow & Gate baby food. You know, the stuff you can just heat up and throw down the baby's throat. Well look, I know it's silly, but we didn't think it through. We must have realised Mme et Msr Johnny Foreigner produced babies from time to time like wot we did, but it just didn't occur to us there would be baby food readily available in French supermarkets. So we took humungous stocks of Cow & Gate's finest and other baby supplies, and the caravan was overloaded with tins, jars and all manner of provisions.

The weather on that trip was boiling hot, and in that sort of sweltering environment, insects and creepy crawlies proliferate. Daniel, who was just a toddler, was more than a little nervous of the majority of them, and on one occasion he pointed a stubby finger at a flying daddy long legs or something or other on the caravan window and shouted: 'Arggh!'

Clive then did something that proves once and for all he could never have been a child psychologist. He approached the dancing winged creature in question and examined it carefully before jumping back and exclaiming: 'Arrgh! it's MAN EATING!' And with that he dashed across the caravan in feigned terror. Holding his hands over his face. Obviously, the poor child then lost it completely and broke down in hysterics. Trevor and I shook our heads in disapproval, but we were also laughing discreetly. Clive's sense of humour was always a bit much for the children, but these days, when he has one of his funny moments they just shake their heads sympathetically, remembering his antics from years past.

When the Paul Ricard meeting was over we all went into Marseilles for a bit of a look around. Our next race was the Spanish Grand Prix which was a two and a half day drive away, so we took the Monday off before getting on our way. I remember us walking along the sea front and having a bit of a row for some long-forgotten reason, as most couples do from time to time. But whatever it was about it didn't dampen our spirits. It was a lovely sunny day and we were out in the sunshine.

Boy was it hot! We experienced a new type of street food, I recall, no doubt a Marseilles delicacy. It can best be described as a loaf of bread, with its middle ripped out and replaced by french fries. Now Marseille is a rough city when all's said and done, and this high-carb treat is probably looked upon as the ultimate in sophisticated fare by soldiers of the Foreign Legion whose HQ is nearby.

Clive was up first the following morning, repeat vomiting into one of the nice flower beds which decorated the Paul Ricard paddock. He was also running a steaming temperature and shivering with cold. Sunstroke was the diagnosis, and Trevor and I loaded the van with bikes, children and what have you, then set off for Spain with our quivering wreck of a rider lying on the back seats of the van wrapped in a blanket. If anything, it was even hotter than the previous day, maybe even the hottest day of the year.

Whenever we lowered the windows to obtain some heat relief, the shivering twerp in the back protested he was cold and demanded we closed them again. We were boiling and it was killing us, but we had to look after him, poor love. This was the man who was going to win us some prize money at the weekend, so we had to make sure he survived.

On that journey down to Spain one of the caravan tyres blew, as they are prone to do when they are used seriously. Let's face it they are designed for occasional trundles to the seaside, perhaps totalling two or three hundred miles a year, not 300 miles a day on steaming tarmac. When a caravan tyre expires at speed, the wheel is usually damaged too, and when you are towing with a van or truck you often don't notice until you are flashed by a fellow road user.

It's not so much of a problem at night as you see sparks trailing behind you in the mirrors, as the wheel rim scrapes and grinds along the ground. I have known flat tyres burst into flames in these circumstances.

Turning off the French autoroute into a small village, we managed to find an obliging and inventive local car mechanic who fitted us up with a replacement wheel of the right stud pattern and fitted with a truck tyre of almost the right size. It worked surprisingly well. In fact it was still on the caravan when we sold it two years later. You can't beat good tyres, and we are both quite fanatical about them these days.

Upon arrival at the Spanish border at the dead of night we were given a bit of a going over by Franco's customs boys. Actually, the General had died a couple of years before and there had been an immediate return to democracy, but this was still well before they were in the EU and fully civilised (!). For a start, they didn't recognise the RAC carnet we used to get the race bikes through customs. Oh no, they had a different plan altogether. We had to follow a lunatic customs officer into the nearby town of Jonquera, where he took us to a friendly 'agent' (or crook), who would relieve us of 600 pesetas and keep the carnets in his safe until we came back to collect them before leaving the country.

It was the dead of night, and we had to wait in a lorry park until the agent opened his office in the morning. I wonder if customs people ever get Christmas cards.

Brown Water

M orning eventually came and the agent duly appeared and opened up, and the dodgy deed was done. The dependable Trevor took over the driving duties once more (I had done most of it the previous night) while our wrecked rider remained prostrate in the back. Daniel watched the world go by from his child seat and Emma, good as gold, slept the day away on a shelf above the rear passenger seat.

On and on we went, grinding our way down to Jarama. In those days the motorway stopped at Zaragoza. After that it was dust roads and the sort of terrain where around every bend you expected to see Clint Eastwood on a mule, or bandits with bad teeth and a big hats, holding you up at gunpoint. 'Hey senor. Hand over ya money ora we blowa your head off!'

Sure enough a couple of riders duly appeared into view, but it was OK they were motorcycle policemen. Actually, not OK: they turned out to be villains after all. Corrupt b*****ds. We were pulled over by these jokers, and they demanded we pay a fine for crossing a double white line. We had done no such thing, of course, but they knew most foreigners wouldn't make too much of a fuss. That we would most likely cough up and get it over with so we could press on.

Targeting Trevor in particular as he was in the driving seat, they kept doing the thumb rubbing across fingers thing, demanding pesetas. Clive, who had been sleeping in the back, heard raised voices and stuck his head out, demanding a 'recibo', or receipt. With that they lost interest and cleared off on their Sanglas 500s. Scumbags!

Arriving at the circuit of Jarama a few kilometres north of Madrid otherwise intact, we found we did not have a confirmed start for the Grand Prix. Never mind, our rider was now back to his impossibly positive self. 'No problem, we'll fix it.' And with that he set about unloading the bikes. After pitching camp, I went to the paddock water tap, and lo! What issued forth was brown. Now I don't care who you are or how robust your digestive system, you do not give a 10-week-old baby and a toddler brown tap water. 'Don't worry we'll fix it.'

Well, Clive and Trevor fixed the start problem and began preparing the bike, but I was still vexed about the water. 'No problem, we'll fix it.' Yes, but when? I had two children to feed and no water. I was hot, tired, and at breaking point. Of course, there were no disposable nappies back then. We were using Terry towelling things that had to be washed in a bucket, but NOT IN BROWN WATER!

I started to get a meal ready for the adults, and in the process got in the way of a blowback from the oven which singed my eyelashes, eyebrows and my hair. I was not happy with my perm as it was, now it was a frightful frizzy mess. I was at the point of losing it. I needed an arm around me, I needed sympathy, I needed love, and most of all I needed water. But they just laughed and said, 'Don't worry, we'll fix it.' 'When!?' 'After practice, we're out next.'

I was screaming inside. They didn't seem to understand. I was so lonely. I was fuming. The water was brown. What's not to understand? Pressure was building but I had a job to do, so on went the professional hat and I grabbed a child under each arm, together with my clipboard and stopwatches, and went to the top of the stand at turn two where I recorded Clive's lap times throughout the session.

That done it was the men's turn to come up with the goods, and we all piled into the van and set off to find a shop. We had never been to Jarama before so we just followed our noses. After a while we spotted what looked like a housing estate, but as we drew nearer we saw a security gate. We had only seen this kind of set up outside military bases in the UK, and it was a little disconcerting, but the estate's security guard paid us no heed anyway as we trundled past him.

After bumping over some sleeping policemen (not real ones, you understand. I'm talking speed bumps) we came across something that looked a little bit like a shop. It was just a corrugated iron shack but posters advertising ice creams (helados) and Omo glued on the side of it gave us a clue. Inside the place there were the usual festering hams these latin heathens generally favour hanging from the roof, but also some of the products we desperately needed. But the proprietor had no English and we only knew half a dozen words of Spanish between us, so after a few minutes of us speaking English in raised voices, as is the classic British way when dealing with Johnny Foreigner, and him looking blank and not a little bored, he handed us over to his ten-year-old son.

And what a good plan that was too because he turned out to be a very bright kid indeed. After we tried a thesaurus of words for water - wasser, vesi, eau, glugg glugg glugg - and acted out drinking the clear stuff with our very best mimes, he calmly said: 'Ah, agua mineral'. By jove, that was it. Of course! From acqua, the latin for water. Bleedin' obvious innit? We bought a couple of cases of bottled water and heaps more stuff as well. What a wonderful, bright, helpful, child. I expect he is a doctor now. He saved my children's lives that weekend anyway. When the Spanish Grand Prix was over, around mid-afternoon on the Sunday, it occurred to me that Spaniards really were a civilised bunch after all. We had half a day off. Wahey! I made my way down from the grandstand as I had done several times over the weekend, dressed, as usual, in a bikini. You have to love central Spain in April! So there I was, baby in my arms, child held by the hand, clip board and stopwatches and other paraphernalia trapped under my arm, and I passed a sidecar crew pitched near us in the paddock. 'Thank you,' someone said. 'What for?' said I. 'You have made our weekend a pleasure as you have walked backwards and forwards in your bikini.' What a lovely thing to say. I like sidecar crews!

Clive had battled to a fine fourth place, having spent much of the race dicing with Giacomo Agostini's younger brother, Felice. But the result didn't come without our accustomed moments of drama. The regulations covering the meeting were written out in Spanish, so we could make neither head nor tail of them, but Arabic numerals were used so at least we could work out the length of our race, or so we thought.

Working on the basis there were 26 laps, the bike was sufficiently fuelled with a bit extra added 'just in case' (Trevor was always very thorough), and the signal board was prepared with a 26 on it (each time Clive came round a lap would be deducted - 25, then 24 and so on). With around ten laps to go Clive decided to ease off in his fight with Felice, to lull the Italian into losing focus a little, before zapping him on the final lap. Saving the best 'til last, as it were, to see young Ago off! At the right time, or so we thought, Trevor signalled 'Last Lap' and Clive really went for it, leaving Ago Minor floundering in his wake, but when Clive approached the start and finish line expecting to see a chequered flag, Trevor gave him another LL signal! 'OK, never mind,' thought our man, 'There's been a bit of a cock up, I'll just give it another hot one!' Felice was even further behind next time round, but there was still no chequered flag. Just a signal from Trev that said: 'L?'

Clive went round again and again and again until the chequered flag was eventually waved after 32 laps! It appeared we had read in the regs that the race would be a minimum of 26 laps. We were lucky (2 and 6 make 8 don't forget) that we had enough fuel in reserve. Fortunately the error gave us all a good laugh, and not the tears that might have flowed had Clive broken down for want of fuel. The early finish to the day's racing gave us time to relax over a pot of tea and plan our next move. We decided to spend a week on the Costa Brava, as our next meeting was in Holland in two weekends' time, but just a three day drive away.

Well, what a great holiday we had (not). A lovely camp site was found, right on the beach, near a Catalonian seaside town called Blanes, but it rained solidly. Hang on! We were in Spain, but suffering day after day of miserable, dreary, relentless, sodding, British-style rain. I was just glad we hadn't booked through Thomas Cook, or we would have had to lynch a rep by way of retribution.

After several days of doing jigsaws and 'brumming' model cars up and down the caravan while the rain drummed down, we decided to move north to a fishing town called Roses. We were still in Spain, but here, at least, the coast was not so 'brave'. We found a pleasant sloping beach and the weather was slightly better. We did a bit of touring round for which, we found a LWB Transit diesel was not the ideal tool. One day we visited a picturesque village accessed from a precipitous clifftop road, and we ended up driving along incredibly narrow village streets. Eventually we could go no further and we had to go most of the way back up in reverse. Still, that's the way adventures often turn out. Not how you imagine them!

The time finally came for us to wend our way up to Holland via the dodgy agent at Jonquera who still held our carnet. But as we left the campsite we caught some overhead wires on the caravan skylight and pulled them down. We left skid marks as we sped away.

Kidnapped!

We were heading for a Dutch city called Tilburg where road races were held on the perimeter road of a holiday park. It was a delightful place called the Beekse Bergen. I recall there was a wooden bridge, which was part of the circuit; there was a lake in the centre of the park with a beach; and there was a municipal zoo. You could hear lions roaring at night sometimes - something I would hear again many years later when we went on a camping trip in the Kruger Park. But that's another story.

We were joined in the Netherlands by our friend and backer, Robin, and I opened my heart to him about how some things just weren't right. For a start, the sleeping arrangements were upsetting me. Like Fletcher in Porridge, Clive had used his old lag status to bag the top bunk, leaving me down below with the offspring. Trevor was billeted in a separate, curtained-off area.

Robin rearranged the accommodation. It was like having a visit from a marriage guidance therapist and I could now sleep with my husband once again. 'Now that's how it should be,' Dr Robin told Clive, and my life got a little bit better. But there was more trauma ahead for the Horton family!

On race day after yet another race win (I was getting a bit blasé about this, to be honest), we lost Daniel! Half the paddock was put on red alert as we desperately searched other team's vans, caravans and awnings. I remember Andrea Herron was very helpful and others too, but no joy. I was in a terrible funk, but then I spotted him in the distance, walking along the beach by the lake on the other side of a high fence. A stranger was holding his hand and they were walking away from me.

Robin saw what I saw and took a running leap at the fence, and having cleared it, and with smoke coming off his shoes, he sprinted over to them and brought Daniel back. Oh my, was I relieved. As it turned out the chap was someone who knew Clive, and he was taking Daniel to 'lost property'. Nevertheless, it was a moment no mother would ever want repeated in any circumstances!

Austria was our next destination, the Salzburgring to be precise. A dangerous race track in a beautiful region of one of the loveliest countries in the world. The only trouble was it was run by former members of the Waffen SS who hated motorcyclists. I came to this conclusion as absolutely nothing they did was designed to help the riders or assist paddock life in any way. Even getting in and out of the circuit involved a documentation checking process akin to that of Stalag Luft 17.

Anyway we got in and scraped enough snow to one side to park up and set up camp, and the following day snow ploughs cleared the white stuff off the race surface so practice could commence. I remember the Dunlop rep pulling at his hair, and saying: 'This is madness. They can't ride in these conditions, the tyres will not get warm enough.' But ride they did, and with snow piled high at the sides of the track, the meeting got underway. Ah well, at least it was something soft for the riders to land on if they fell down. Cue a verse of Eric Idle's 'Always Look on the Bright Side of Life' from a film of that year, Monty Python's Life of Brian.

A local we chatted to said the weather was set to improve for race day. 'Tomorrow you will not believe your eyes,' he said. And sure enough race day dawned bright and sunny and soon the snow was all but gone. Sadly our rider crashed out at about half distance, but the good news was he was not really hurt, just stunned. A few days later we came across a spectacular sequence of photographs of the crash, caught by an alert lensman, which had been printed in an Italian bike magazine.

My next mission was to get his lordship to the airport. He was entered in a race at Oulton Park the following day, which was a Bank Holiday Monday, on the stalwart little Fosters Honda. That done, Trevor and I had to get the team to south-west France where the French Grand Prix was taking place the following weekend at Nogaro-en-Armagnac. Clive would rejoin us there, arriving under his own steam after Monday's English meeting.

Trevor and I drove for about two days solid, although we did call in for lunch and a quick look around in Monaco, and we drove our rig around the famous street circuit.

As we got nearer to Nogaro, the roads turned into some of the roughest we had ever come across, bouncing the caravan around like a toy, and when we finally arrived at our destination and had a look inside it, we were met by a scene of utter devastation. Jars of baby food had jumped out of the cupboards and off the shelves, smashing and leaving chips in the melamine table top. What a pigsty we had to clear up when, tired from travelling, all we wanted to do was go to bed. Sometimes life is not fair.

When Clive arrived a day or so later, he appeared as we entertained some visitors in our caravan, and we were all sitting around chatting in a bit of a smog, as some of those present, including me, were indulging our tobacco habits. Well, he went berserk and threw everyone out for smoking in his home.

He was hopping mad - as mad as a box of frogs, in fact. He had brought a very large toy car with him - a present for Daniel's birthday, which was the event we were all celebrating when he appeared and blew his top. Ah well, maybe he'd had a tough journey. In the race he crashed out on the second corner of the first lap. Hey ho, nobody's perfect!

It was then back to the Netherlands for a race meeting in the only hilly part of that famously flat country. The circuit in the town of Heerlen in the province of Limburg was on public roads and we parked up in a makeshift paddock just a few meters from a graveyard (reassuring!). Typically, for Holland, it immediately started to rain so we sought shelter in the caravan. As the rain drummed relentlessly on the roof we hatched a plan. Having spotted a launderette, we decided to use the day to catch up with our washing backlog. I was sick and tired of hand-washing filthy underwear, whether that of babies, or mechanics and riders.

It was my first and last visit to one of these places. Clearly, they are only for the very wealthy, or those who are idle and have plenty of time to kill. Still, it kept us under cover and out of the bad weather.

Clive won his race on the Saturday. Racing usually takes place on a Saturday in the Netherlands, a hang over from more religious times, I would think. The track was a simple street circuit and the riders blasted up one side of a dual carriageway, went through the aforementioned graveyard, and then flew down the other side of the carriageway, and that was about it! A win is a win though, and we were chuffed to bits. I think it was the only time the meeting was ever run.

Mettet, in Belgium was our next destination. It was only a short drive away, but we planned to go via Ostend, as Trevor was suffering with painful toothache and he needed to get back to the UK and get it fixed.

Toothache

Doesn't he look smug. 1977 had its ups and downs but also delivered the first Honda MT125 Championship. Clive on the final Brands Hatch podium with race winner Bernard Murray and Honda's Gerald Davidson

S unday was deadly quiet in Holland and Belgium and Trevor was as miserable as sin. We stopped to eat in a countryside restaurant and the Horton family had a jolly nice meal, but poor ol' Trev wasn't interested. His tooth was sucking at his spirit. Suddenly, Clive had an idea! Oh God help us all.

Several months before he had met a female Belgian spectator called Dora, who had said, if ever he was in her neck of the woods he should pop in and look her up. Actually, I think she took a bit of a shine to Clive, especially when she found out he was a super-glamorous professional motorcycle racer. I didn't trust her an inch (or should that be a centimetre).

Anyway, this Dora woman and her husband, Richard, ran a pub in Belgium called The Robin Hood. I am not making this up! We were not far away from it, so perhaps we could go and see if Dora could help us find a dentist, suggested Clive. Also, we were short of Belgian francs. Maybe she could oblige us and swap us some for our Heerlen prize money, which was in guilders.

We found the pub easily enough, but despite its village location, and the fact it was Sunday, the place was heaving with teenagers and rollacking loud music was booming out of it. Rather unexpected, but perhaps this is what they get up to after church?

Clive recognised Richard behind the bar and shouted 'Dora?' over the din, only to receive a dirty look in return. Then a young woman tapped Clive on the shoulder and steered him back outside. We then learned that Dora had recently run off with one of the pub's customers. Oh dear, Clive's cunning plan had failed, but maybe help was at hand after all. Our informant was an intelligent, helpful girl, who spoke impeccable English. She took us to the local bank manager's house and asked him to fix us up with some Belgian francs. No problem, and with good humour, he did this for us. Amazingly, he took us to his bank, opened its safe right in front of us, and traded the banknotes.

Unfortunately she wasn't quite so good at solving the toothache problem. All she could suggest was going back to the pub for a glass or two of Underberg, a traditional Belgian cure-all which tastes not unlike WD40. Trevor didn't fancy this so, defeated, we went back to plan A, and continued on to Ostend.

Now this brings back a memory. A few years before, Clive and I had sat in the very waiting room where we now dropped Trevor off. Too early for our ferry on that occasion, we decided to have a cup of coffee; and while we sipped our drinks we chatted about nothing in particular and stared at the walls, as you do. I recall we were bringing home a good few quid in prize money that day after a foreign race meeting, probably about £100. It was a good haul in those days and we felt rather pleased with ourselves.

Presently a young fellow drew up noisily in a less than pristine Ford Escort, and then came in and sat down with a cup of coffee at an adjacent table. When I went to use the powder room, Clive told me he sidled over, sat in my seat and asked if we would be interested in posing for some photographs. You know the sort of thing, nudge nudge, wink wink.

'There will be some money in it for you,' he added, hoping this would tip the balance. Clive glanced at the man's scabby Escort outside, cast an eye over the fellow, and, surreptitiously checking the wad of notes in his left buttock pocket, said: 'Er, no. I don't think she will be up for it, thanks mate.' The budding porn magnate had left when I returned, and Clive related these goings on. I said I was surprised he had even considered it! Too right I would never be up for that sort of thing. 'Oh! well that wasn't the reason I passed it up. It was the cash in my pocket. I looked at his scruffy car and thought there obviously can't be much money in pornography, I might get bashed on the head and robbed.' Thanks Clive.

The sweet smell of....hope

The Mettet weekend was completed without Trevor's expert help, although we did pressgang a fellow competitor to pit for us during the race while I stood on the back straight, away from the start and finish line, doing my lap scoring and looking after the children.

Clive led from the start, and soon had the race comfortably under control, but as he came past me on the last lap he had been demoted to second, 100 yards in arrears. What in heaven's name had occurred? It appears as he crossed the line to start the last lap the engine had mysteriously died, but as soon as the next rider passed it had fired up again (it must have been missing Trevor!), so Clive was now in hot pursuit. He regained the lead just before the finish line; what a relief! Our temporary crew member was dead chuffed: 'I've never pitted for a winner before,' he said. 'But I can't take that sort of drama every week!'

A funny story about young Daniel. When we travelled in the van, Dan used to sit in his little car seat on the passenger side of the cab, next to the door, and on the continent that put him in the middle of the road, facing the traffic. Of course, on long runs we had to entertain him. 'What's that car coming the other way, Daniel?' He'd say: 'It's a Fiat.' 'Not a Seat?' 'No, no, no, it's a Fiat.' And invariably he was right! How did he know? He was only two. He could never tell us, but part of it became clear when we were wandering around a car park one day and I realised he knew all the badges. It also amused us that after a long stint driving around Europe, when we rolled off the ferry back in England he said. 'Hey, how come I'm next to the pavement!'

We returned home for a small break before the TT in the Isle of Man, and to pick up Trevor of course. For that year's races we had entries in what over there is called the Lightweight TT (250cc) the Junior TT (350cc) and the 1000cc Classic TT, for which we would again use Robin's TZ350 Yamaha.

For TT fortnight we rented a Victorian house somewhere in the bowels of Douglas, a huge place that would accommodate not only our team and family but also Clive's mum and dad. Yes, a fortnight living with the mother-in-law! Things worked reasonably well though, it must be said. She would get up and sort Trevor's breakfast out for those God forsaken dawn practice sessions, giving me an extra half hour lay-in. The meeting was fairly uneventful overall, everything going reasonably according to plan, and we had decent results in the races except for the Junior, where, during the pit stop for refuelling, the engine mountings were found to be broken.

Pitstops at the TT are not the wham-bam-thank-you-ma'm affairs you might expect. They are actually fairly leisurely, and the standard issue re-fuelling system supplied in those days was quite slow. This allowed time for the technical officials to have a quick look over the bike, trying to spot any potentially hazardous problems and breakages. If they find any, enforced retirement is usually the result, and often the rider has to be physically pulled off the bike, so pumped full are they of biochemicals, such as endorphins, dopamine, serotonin, and adrenaline. They want to continue, and are not at all rational in the moment.

Because of the broken engine mountings the 350cc engine had to be placed in the 250cc rolling chassis. This was straightforward enough as it was a virtually identical bike, but with only a single front disc brake. In the 1000cc 'Classic' - a great event - Clive was probably riding at his best level ever in the Island. It was certainly the fastest he ever went there, recording a lap speed of over

106mph. He ended up 11th, I think, but that was very good indeed against 500cc, 750cc and 1000cc bikes, and considering that during the final lap the brakes were overheated and essentially shot.

When it came to the Swedish and Finnish Grands Prix later in the year, because of cost I was considered 'not wanted on voyage'. It would be only rider and mechanic on that long trip and I was as cross as hell. Why was I now considered persona non grata in the team of which I thought I was an important member? Had I not given up all my money, time, effort, and indeed my life, to this enterprise? Had I not shared in all the highs and lows to this point? To be not wanted at this crucial and exciting stage of the season hurt very badly and I made my opinion felt. Clive and I parted company on poor terms during a race meeting at Snetterton. Here, the boys joined up with another team to cut costs even further, setting off in their transporter towing our caravan, going to two new countries, on a thrilling adventure (it was not all work) that I was to be no part of.

I drove our Transit home accompanied by a two-year-old and a six-month-old, returning with no mate to an empty house, feeling guilty about our bad parting but still angry at him for discarding me. Then of course there was the worry he might not come home at all. He was in a high risk business after all, and we had already lost several friends to the sport.

Over the next few days I calmed down and started to look forward to him telephoning me. What a waste of time that was! He did phone just after the first race, but only for about 30 seconds. (He never had enough money for phone calls, which also made me mad.) but it was good to hear his voice, and to know he was safe.

I muddled through the next week, stupidly thinking Clive would phone again, but as you will have guessed by now, there was no chance of that. He did call after the Finnish GP but that was a repeat of the short-lived Swedish scenario. Then, a day or so later I received a post card which read, 'I'm coming home, get your knickers off'. Clive has never been known for mincing his words, and considering he had been surrounded for days by the legendary Nordic nymphs, and was in the company of blokes all no doubt egging each other on, I suppose I felt rather flattered. Knowing he was safely on his way back, I could really look forward to us being reunited, and to being back in the team at the British Grand Prix at Silverstone.

Clive returned having had a reasonably productive time in the lands of the midnight sun, gaining valuable world championship points at both events. Our tally was mounting. It was very important that we should accumulate enough points to finish in the top ten in the world standings in order to be guaranteed, not only a start at each event the following year, but £200 in start money as well. Finishing 11th would mean nothing.

Postcard not withstanding, the panties stayed firmly on. You can't be seen to give in too easily can you! The Silverstone event got underway and our relationship soared along with it. We had many visitors from well-wishers and trade reps to our garage, which was actually our TT tent. We were using it to avoid the hustle and bustle of the pit lane, feeling being in that febrile area was not conducive to good mental preparation for a big event.

One of our visitors was a chap lugging a plastic bag full of various sorts of brake pads. He asked Clive if he'd care to try a set in practice. 'Sure, no problem.' Just typical. The trial turned out successful, in as much as we would use them in the race, and the bloke with the plastic bag turned out to be the MD of a British brake pad manufacturing company called EBC, namely Andy Freeman. Over the next few years Andy became a good friend and a significant contributor to the team's efforts. Another example of the importance of not letting appearances influence judgement of a person. It is their character that matters.

Silverstone in August can be all sorts of things weather-wise. Hot as hell, cool and grey, wet and windy, or quite likely all three. This time would be no different. Qualifying was mainly dry and sunny, but on the Sunday morning of the race the circuit was wet with rain. The track was making an effort to dry, but the sky was threatening. The 125cc bikes in those days didn't use treadless slick tyres, so at least tyre choice was not a major headache.

Clive started in his usual mediocre manner, but he soon got a move on and started getting near the front. I was lap timing and giving Trevor the info he needed for the pit board, and we were chucking numbers down like billyo as he climbed to sixth, fifth, then the giddy heights of fourth, so that with just a few laps remaining he had the reigning world champion Eugenio Lazzarini directly in front of him in third. Thierry Espie on the works Motobecane was further ahead in second place, and the works bike of Angel Nieto was out in front. Clive passed Lazzarini for third place - this was getting really exiting now - then Espie's bike dramatically expired and we were up to second.

And that is how the podium looked at the end. The world champion elect stood on the top step, the current champ was to the left of him in third, and my bloke was there on the right. An Italian magazine also gave him the accolade of the hero of the race. (But that's only because they didn't know him like I did.)

Due to the ongoing sketchy wet/dry conditions the 250cc bike was fitted with intermediate tyres which turned out to be the wrong choice as the track dried out, so Robin's Yamaha was retired. It was, however, a great meeting for us and for our points tally in the 125cc class, and therefore my housekeeping money prospects for the following year were looking bright indeed.

Mind you, being so successful in the wet meant Clive now considered himself a bonafide 'Rain God'. Isn't it strange how readily men can promote themselves to deity on any flimsy evidence that suits them at the time.

John Player
BRITISH GRAND PRIX
Silverstone 5th - 6th August 1978

1978 John Player British Grand Prix

125 cc Race

Psn.	No.	Name	Time	Speed	KPH
1st	3	Angel Nieto	44.51.08	93.97	151.22
2nd	31	Clive Horton	45.08.10	93.37	
3rd	2	Eugenio Lazzarini	45.12.28	93.23	
4th	38	Thierry Espie	45.20.98	92.93	
5th	8	Hans Müller	45.31.75	92.57	
6th	7	Stefan Dorflinger	45.32.02	92.56	
7th	17	Bam Carlsson	45.36.45	92.40	
8th	39	Yves Dupont	45.52.99	91.85	
9th	4	Jean-Louis Guignabodet	46.01.47	91.57	
10th	20	Felice Agostini	46.01.73	91.56	
11th	43	Carl Fuchs	46.35.48	90.46	
12th	30 (23 laps)	Cees Van Dongen	45.16.45		
13th	34	Daniel Meyer	45.29.60		
14th	47	Ernst Fagerer	45.36.29		
15th	24	Patrick Herouard	46.12.73		
16th	29 (22 laps)	Jan Ubels	44.57.65		
17th	36	Alain Pellet	44.57.95		

Fastest Lap : No. 2 Eugenio Lazzarini 1.42.22   103.08 mph 165.88 kph

Surely things could only get better?

Time for a reality check

After Silverstone we moved on to one of the international money earning events. We are not talking really big money by the way, but we were grateful for the odd extra £100 or so for subsistence. This one was at a street circuit not far from Bruges in Belgium at a village called Sint Joris Ten Distel, a right old mouthful, but still miles away from Llanfairpilwingilgilgillygoch-gochgoch. Thank God we didn't have to go there for a race meeting! But sometimes these foreigners, I ask you.

Anyway, there was no 125cc race at this Belgian public roads event but we were entered for the 250cc event. Clive qualified in 32nd place, absolutely hopeless, right on the back of the grid. As the riders took their places for the start there was a massive cloudburst and in seconds the place was awash. Riders using Michelins quickly fitted the French factory's special new rain tyres, but as we were using tyres by Dunlop, who did not make a suitable rain tyre at that time, all we could do was fit their intermediates. You could almost see the halo over our beaming 'Rain God'. He was very happy, radiant even. The race got underway and after just one lap Clive was up to eighth place, although I could hardly see him the spray was so intense. But that glimpse was the last I did see of him for something like four hours of absolute mental agony.

Riders were aquaplaning and crashing out all over the place, my 'Rain God' among them. After much running around, those of us in the pit lane learned that several riders had been hurt, some very badly. There was talk of broken arms, broken backs, and serious head injuries, and what's more no-one knew who had which injury, or where any of them had been taken. It was absolute bedlam and mostly in Flemish, and as the circuit roads were closed we could not escape the paddock if we wanted to. We were stuck on an island surrounded by a sea of high speed madness.

Clive claims he'd hatched a plan to catch the leading group. The main straight was not so much a straight as a long radius curve, and he thought if he could hold the throttle fully open as he drove through it, he would then be right amongst them. He regained consciousness in the bottom of a drainage ditch that lined the road. His legs were sticking out at very odd angles and he thought, 'Oh my God this time I must have broken something.' He was extracted by the trackside helpers, or marshals as they are called, and stretchered off to a white bell tent in the middle of a soggy field. The Crimea, 1854 was the thought that struck him, apparently!

Inside the tent he was placed on a hard worktop and inspected by a medic, and moments later another British rider, Clive Padgett from Batley was bought in and laid on the floor. He was bleeding from his forehead and decidedly confused, but he recognised my Clive and asked in his delirious state, 'Wer a weh Clive? Wer a weh?' (Apologies but that is the best I can do to establish the young fellow was speaking in his native Yorkshire accent.) Clive told him they were in the middle of a field in Belgium and tried to be reassuring. 'Ow am a?' he enquired. Clive peered down at him, saw his messy state and cringed (he is a bit of a squeamish tart). 'No worries mate,' he said (he had lately been keeping company with Australians). 'You look fine.' He was lying.

Trawling through the paddock trying to get information I bumped into another Sue, this one being the girlfriend of the afore-mentioned young Padgett and in a complete state of limbo like me. Then we were approached by one of the other competitors, who helped us tremendously. This kind man took us under his wing, borrowed a car, weaved his way through woods, fields and lanes, taking no nonsense from anyone who got in the way, shouting abuse where necessary in French and English. Our helper was actually an Australian of French/Moroccan decent married to an English girl - quite a combination of cultures! He even spoke French to his children while his wife spoke to them in English, and I suppose they have turned out to be very special as well. Thank you, Vic Soussan.

When we arrived at the hospital no one knew anything about our men. Vic's perfect French helped considerably (most Belgians are fluent in Flemish and French) but communication was still patchy. At last we discovered there were three injured riders; one with a broken arm, one with an undiagnosed back injury, and one with a serious spinal injury. But no one knew where they were. In fact, we had arrived at the hospital before they did. Eventually the ambulances arrived and the patients were put in different rooms, although confusion still reigned especially with there being two back injuries and two Clives. And the fact there were also two Sues didn't help matters either. The situation started to sort itself out when we were asked to visit the 'bodies' to identify them. Their words not mine, and thank goodness just an unfortunate miscommunication. There had been no fatalities.

I found my Clive in a corridor lying on a trolley. He'd been there for some time and was beginning to get a bit fed up. He told us all he could remember, and that he had suspected broken vertebrae and a broken ankle, 'But that's without any X-rays', added Clive, 'It's only the on-site analysis of the doctor who turned up at the trackside Crimea tent on a motorbike. He could be a medical genius or a complete drama queen.' Clive reckoned on the latter, and encouraged me to take him straight back to the paddock. I thought just in case the guy did know his stuff we should stay right where we were. After X-rays it turned out the motorcycling doctor was indeed 100% genius, and Clive was kept in. It turned out Clive was the least damaged of the threesome. The other Sue's Clive, was far more badly hurt. His head injury, notwithstanding the bloody appearance, was actually not so bad. It was his broken arm that was the more serious injury, and when the doctor explained to his girlfriend that he would lose it, things looked very grim indeed. Fortunately there was something of a loss in translation and what the doc meant was not that it would be amputated, but that he may lose the full use of it, and sadly he did. Just 19 and only one good arm, simply tragic. Worse yet was that the other young man of the three, Australian Ray Quincey, had been rendered paraplegic at only 20 years of age.

I returned exhausted to the paddock. It was now evening, and as I'd hoped, Clive's brother David, who had come with us 'just for the fun of it', had fed, watered, and then put to bed our two young children (pretty impressive for a 14-year-old), while Trev had recovered the wreckage of the bike and loaded everything up ready for us to move on.

Thankfully transport and mobile-accommodation for Team Horton had moved on by 1978. Clive with Trevor Smedley

An unexploded bomb

T he following day we moved into the hospital grounds and camped alongside the other affected families, feeling once again like gypsies. It was a steaming hot August day and a canal ran adjacent to the hospital. It was Bruges after all, the 'Venice of Belgium'. It was a wonderful breeding ground for mosquitos, and boy did we suffer, particularly poor little Emma. At least we could swat a few away, she just had to take it. While we were being bitten to blazes, Clive was comfortably tucked up in the most luxurious hospital any of us had ever seen. It was fantastic. Even the carpets ran a few feet up the walls. And the neat plaster they put on his ankle was similarly perfect - a work of art.

Fortunately he wasn't having too good a time. He was immobile in bed to prevent his back being disturbed, and he shared a room with three others, one a builder who had fallen off a roof and broken both his ankles, and two old duffers, one of whom was an Alzheimer sufferer who continually shat the bed, often immediately after the nurses had changed him. In the end they fixed him up with an adult nappy and put cot sides on his bed to prevent him wandering about.

But these measures were to no avail, unfortunately. Clive said: 'In the dead of night I'd hear the sound of tearing Velcro as he removed the nappy, then the creak of the bed and padding footsteps as he clambered over the side and pottered around.' In the end the staff fixed Clive up with an emergency device complete with panic button, and when he pressed it they would come rushing in, switching the lights on to reveal a geriatric nutcase wandering about the ward with faeces hanging out of his crack.

89

This silly old sod really upset the other old guy in the bed next to him, particularly when he pissed in a waste basket on one of his outings. All we could make out of the outraged chap's presumably Flemish rant was: 'Ech bin pissen int der flashen, das vuil bassen!', which we took to mean something like: 'It is the height of bad manners when one pisses in a waste basket!'

During the day the boys and our small children went to the beach only a few miles away for an outing, while I stayed behind to sort out the position regarding medical insurance. I phoned the insurance company in England and they were very helpful, explaining in detail the cover we had, and the choices and options open to us, including the number of X-rays, the charges for drugs and for the ankle plaster, and how many nights in the hospital we were entitled to receive.

I went to the hospital administration department and told them that if they expected to be paid for all their efforts, we needed to get Clive back to England by Friday at the latest because that was when our cover would be used up. They weren't at all happy and insisted on proof an ambulance had been organised to meet us off the boat in Dover which would transfer the patient the 200 miles to Derby. If we proved it, they said, they in turn would fix us up with a vacuum stretcher and a nurse who would escort us all the way across to Dover in case of any emergencies. Soon it was all arranged, and all in all the Belgians provided an absolutely fantastic service.

Meanwhile, we had to see out a few more days in mosquitoville. Overall, though, we made the best of this set-back and as far as possible we enjoyed our short stay. The other Clive's dad, Peter Padgett, and our Trevor took young David out on the town, and between them they got the 14-year-old drunk (!), while I popped in and out visiting Clive on a regular basis. I even took him his drink of Horlicks last thing at night.

The male nurse enjoyed the trip to Dover, spending some of the time in the bar with Trevor, and he filled us in with what Clive's injuries meant long term. The two crushed vertebrae in his back would not cause problems once healed, but the ankle would be forever weakened, something he would have to live with for the rest of his life. So far this prediction has been bang on.

We were well looked after on the ship by someone in a smart uniform decorated with a kilogram of gold braid. He looked like an admiral but I guess he was the purser. He loaded us on first, fixed us up with a cabin, and fed us all at no charge. Townsend Thoresen scored big points with us that day, and from then on we always sailed with them whenever crossing the channel, right up until their demise following the Zebrugge disaster.

Back in Blighty, Clive had to spend the night in Dover Hospital before the journey up to Derby. What a contrast to the wonderful new, modern, luxurious building he had been in in Bruges. This was a converted workhouse, and his lovely clean ward for four patients was swapped for a Victorian one housing 24. It was like something out of 'Carry on Doctor' or 'Only When I Laugh', and there was something typically British about it. Our workhouses were built in the eighteenth and nineteenth centuries, but we Brits like to hang on to stuff. The staff were great, though to be fair, just as they had been in Belgium.

Not having 'been' for several days, Clive was having trouble with an ever inflating stomach. He explained his problem to a doctor who examined him by tapping on his tummy which reverberated like a kettledrum. His prescription? A bile bean. 'Jesus God in heaven,' exclaimed Clive, he's just played my stomach like the timpanist on

Ravel's Balero and then he offers me a flaming bile bean!' Our disgruntled and bloated rider was returned to Derby Royal the following day by estate car ambulance, while we followed with our racing rig.

Being a bit of a local celebrity, Clive was given a private room at the Royal, and as soon as possible after being installed he managed to convey to a nurse that he was concerned about his stomach, which was still expanding and surely approaching nuclear meltdown. Well, lets face it, he had been flat on his back for seven days now, and since the age of two we humans have been training our bodies not to 'go' when we are laid down. Consequently he hadn't 'been' for nearly a week and was due to explode at any moment.

The nurse took action. Did she mess around with a bile bean? Oh no. Celebrity or not, effective evacuation required subjugation and humiliation, and she immediately shoved a powerful suppository up his bottom. Low! The lock gates of hell were opened and a ghastly torrent gushed forth. A tad embarrassing it may have been but Clive didn't care. Down went the swelling and he was soon smiling again.

Soon after this the local paper sent a photographer to take his picture, much to the matron's disapproval. He was seen as a returning hero, not the idiot that he really was for riding too fast and crashing an aquaplaning motorcycle.

When he was released from hospital, we went to watch a race meeting at Scarborough, and during the journey across to the Yorkshire coast he kept gripping the seat as we approached a hazard or went round a corner, and I realised he was damaged mentally by the crash. It wasn't my driving I assure you, he was actually struggling with something in his head.

Fortunately he soon overcame this problem. Time, as they say, is a great healer, and we all began eagerly looking forward to the Donington Park International, our next race meeting as competitors. But before that the plaster would have to be removed from his ankle, and his back was far from fully fixed.

Realising perhaps how fortunate he had been, Clive decided to make himself a back protector before his return to the tracks. Using an old shirt, a glass fibre kit and some chicken wire, we made a fibreglass mould of his back while he sat in a racing crouch. He remained in position on the bike until the resin had set, then we cleaned and polished the thing and gave it to a professional fibreglass worker who made a back protector from this mould. The plan worked and the end product was something he wore for the rest of his career.

We should have done it before as we'd had plenty of warning. Our best man, Adrian Drew (Mallet Boy you may recall), injured his back just a few days after our wedding as the result of a crash at Brands Hatch, and he has been confined to a wheelchair ever since. One of our heroes is Adrian. It is remarkable to see how he copes and what he will attempt, often with the help of nutter Clive. Escalators hold no fear for him, a tramp through the snow around New York's Central Park has also been successfully attempted, as has a horse and carriage ride in the same location (not easy, when your legs cannot be controlled). The Empire State building has been scaled, and the Twin Towers were similarly nothing to him. What a guy.

The plaster was finally removed back at the hospital, much to my relief - he had been threatening to do it himself - and it was on a very weak and wobbly leg that Clive hobbled around the paddock at Donington Park. Physiotherapy had only just begun and we had to lift him on and off the bike. He broke down in practice which is the only time I can remember a bike prepared by Trevor ever stopping. It was only a flat battery but it meant he had no qualifying time and had to start from the back of the grid.

Never mind! Clive soon hacked his way into second place, catching the leader hand over fist, and we all thought he had the race in the bag, but on the last lap, a back marker got in the way leaving him 50 yards to make up braking for the last corner. He managed 49 of them but had to settle for second place and a new lap record. He confessed later he was prepared to knock the other guy off if he had no other option. You do have to start thinking racing motorcyclists are a bit crazy. There he was, just out of hospital, still injured, and yet quite plainly prepared to get stuck right back in! Racing and winning is genuinely that important to them. It's absolute madness. Impossible to comprehend.

Clive on his way to 2ⁿᵈ place in the Vladivar 250cc race

Wolfy? No, not the one on the TV

During Clive's hospitalisation the final Grand Prix of the year had taken place, and as luck would have it we ended up tenth in the overall standings - the minimum we needed to receive the guaranteed start money that would enable us to compete in Grand Prix the following season.

The end of that first Grand Prix adventure had been tough, and things got even tougher the closer we got to the beginning of the next racing season. The Brader brothers pulled out of the sport due to some sort of domestic dispute. We bought the Transit from Wide Range Engineering but their race support was withdrawn, due to the shareholders having found out how much it had cost the firm the previous year. We were left with good old reliable Robin and his TZ Yamahas, and that was it.

But Clive wanted to be world 125cc champion and he thought he knew how to do it, so he took a bag of money (about £4,000), drove across to Italy and tried to buy an engine directly from the MBA factory. They wouldn't sell him one, which was something of a blow, but a deal was done in the end. He was allowed to take an engine away with him, but he was instructed to pay for it at the company's official importers in England (this must be the only time Italians have ever behaved with such propriety).

Clive took the engine but rather than heading straight home he dropped it off with ace tuner Harald Bartol over the border in Austria. Bartol claimed to be able to extract 40bhp from an MBA 125, fully five more bhp than an engine in standard factory tune. Our engine was duly dropped off and we looked forward to getting it back a couple of months later, it having been made fifteen percent more powerful.

We were now totally skint and didn't yet have a motorcycle to put the engine into. Up stepped Ken Foster, the man who was still backing us in the 125 Honda series. Good old Ken, and thanks too to our mutual friend Bill Bristow who, it must be said, leant on Ken more than a little on our behalf. Clive specified what the rolling chassis needed to be like, Bill drew it, Spondon Engineering built it, Clive and Trevor put it together, and Ken signed the cheques. The wheels were to be extra special and required hubs made from chunks of magnesium billet. That's where I come in to the sorry tale. A six inch diameter billet of this expensive metal was needed for the job, and someone had to collect it from Birmingham. Clive had taken a job (so we could eat, you understand) and was not allowed to have any time off, so it was down to me to fetch this precious material.

The weather was foul and I had no idea where I was going, but I battled through snow, sleet and wind, made it there successfully, and returned with my special cargo which was then taken to a machine shop to be turned into wheel hubs. Sadly, after a couple of weeks, it was discovered the engineers there had not managed to make the high spec items they should have. They had made junk. So enter stage left once again Sue's Pony Express. This time, if anything, the weather was worse, but the wheels needed to be built and I was the woman to get the billet. Nothing would stand in my way, and I completed the mission once again.

Next the 'improved' engine needed to be fetched from Harald Bartol, so Clive, Bill and Trevor set off for snowy Austria in the Transit van. It was February and it was very, very cold. So cold, in fact, the radiator had to be muffed to prevent cold air over cooling the engine, and to keep the heater working. At times, as they pushed on into Europe, there were lorries parked in mountain lay-bys with open fires burning under their fuel tanks to prevent the diesel from turning into jelly.

At Harald's workshop the engine wasn't quite ready so they had to spend the night in the neighbourhood Post House, All towns and villages in Austria have a 'Post', often the first hotel to have been built in the town, and probably a throw-back to the coaching days of yore. They are more B&Bs than hotels really, and jolly good value too. They all shared a room.

Before retiring, and as we were more than a little bit skint, Clive decided to fill the van up with some cheap red diesel available from one of Harald's farmer friends. Our Transit had two fuel tanks, but they weren't all that well balanced, and occasionally the breather pipe of one of them would drip fuel, so we seldom used them both. But on this occasion the fuel was so cheap Clive went for it, probably banking on having enough heavy oil to get them right back to Calais, all for next to nothing.

Then, when the dodgy deed was done, the boys spent a couple of hours in the village nightclub chatting to one of Tom Heron's mechanics, Pete. A night club in a village? More a disco in reality, I suppose. Pete was a really nice bloke, and it was tragic that he would die a terrible death later that same year. He had been driving a race team's artic and had a puncture on the M1 on a really filthy night. He stepped out to inspect the damage and was drawn under the wheels of a passing lorry, sucked there by the vacuum caused by its draught. What cruel luck. Life can be a b****rd. You are lucky if you survive it!

Having left the club they parked the van in deep snow in the village square near the Post and went to bed. Breakfast the next morning was a continental job and not a particularly exciting affair. You could never call a continental breakfast sumptuous in my opinion, and often more a duty than a pleasure. Give me a British breakfast any day! You can eat enough to last all day at some of our hostelries! Anyway, after eating their cheese and ham or whatever, the lads went out to the van only to see it sitting on a sea of red snow. It was obvious what had happened and they lit out before officialdom turned up to ask awkward questions.

The engine was collected later that afternoon and they set off back home, but by the time they reached Stuttgart they were all totally exhausted and could drive no further, so they sought out beds for the night. Everywhere was full, even the posh gaffs, which shows how desperate they were. Trevor was the designated German speaker - he had studied it a bit - and he was sent into each establishment in turn to enquire. The last place they picked looked more of a boozer than a decent overnight and sure enough Trev come out with a shoulder shrug. But this time he had an effusive new friend in tow who offered to put them all up at his home. They refused his generosity and thanked him kindly, but he would not take no for an answer. Probably because he was sodden with drink. This chap introduced himself as Wulf, vis a vee! and spoke rather good, if heavily accented American English, which he had learned from GI's stationed in Germany, and for whom he drove for a living.

Wulf persuaded them to follow him and drove off in his big American car. So we had a professional chauffeur, absolutely hammered, swerving down narrow city streets in a car that was much too big to fit down them, followed by three somewhat reluctant and exhausted Englishmen. They did consider veering off and giving him the slip, but they were simply too knackered to function at that level of initiative. Finally he slowed, and it soon became obvious his destination was a grim-looking block of flats.

Yet deeper gloom descended on the musketeers as they parked the van in this bleak hell hole, worried about leaving their vehicle unattended and fearing especially for the valuable cargo inside it. Reluctantly, but dutifully, they followed Wulf into an austere block of apartments, and then into a lift. Moments later Wulf fell through the door of his tiny apartment and introduced them to his sulky teenage children and his angry looking wife, who immediately ushered him into a back room for a good, dragon-like toasting. There were raised voices, but all in German, of course.

While Wulfy was getting his ears bashed, the musketeers sat in the lounge watching incomprehensible TV with the teens. They kept themselves amused, laughing their stupid heads off, attempting to read the Deutsche TV Times, looking for the German version of 'Kreuz wegs' unt 'Korronation Strasse'. Much fun was had by all, to the extent they were verging on hysterics.

Wulfy emerged from the back room looking suitably admonished, but nonetheless said: 'Come on my friends, let's go for a drink!' The trio exchanged astonished looks. My goodness wasn't he already full to capacity? The last thing this guy needed was more booze. Nevertheless they all trooped out and climbed into his loon-mobile, whereupon he drove off like a man possessed, the huge car rolling wildly in the corners as only an American car can, before arriving at what could only be described as a working man's club or perhaps the German Legion?

The Englanders were introduced to the incumbents, all rough looking, chunky-bellied types, the majority wearing wife-beater vests. There must have been twenty or so. One was a policeman, explained Wulf, another a magistrate, and a third, equally incredibly, the chief of police. Just why a senior policeman chose to dress in a Rab C Nesbit outfit during his evenings off, was never explained. All this nonsense was surely a complete fiction intended to loosen the bowels of the visitors. The boys in turn played their part and pretended to be suitably impressed.

The thing that did help their digestive throughput, however, was when the men all stood up and sang a hearty rendition of Deutschland Uber Alles, complete with the classic straight right arm salute! It was all designed to intimidate the Englanders, of course, and one look at the daft, pained grins on the faces of the interlopers would tell you the job was complete. Maybe Wifey had sent Wulfy out with a job to do, and he vos only obeyink ze orders, so perhaps it wasn't all his fault. Actually, when you think about it from her point of view, it all makes sense. Her drunken idiot of a husband had just brought three total strangers into their home, and two of them were big, burly lads. Absolute madness and not a thing anyone would do in a sober state. Putting the frighteners on them would keep them in their place.

When they all returned to the flat, Wulfy turfed his poor son out of his bed to sleep with his sister (probably illegal, even in Germany), and gave the boy's room to the guests. The mattress was on the floor and touched the walls on each side, and all three lay down to sleep with the biggest two on the outsides and Clive sandwiched in the centre. They couldn't sleep, even though they were absolutely all in by now. They just lay giggling hysterically in total disbelief at the situation, not letting up for an hour or so until they were finally empty of all the emotional chemicals that had set alight in their brains. They did not see Wulf in the morning as he had had an early start, but before retiring for the night he had asked what they wanted for breakfast. 'Oh nothing thanks, we will be ok,' they had said. But he had become cross at this and told them there will be ze scrambled eggs. His wife would cook ze scrambled eggs, ja? And she did too, though with little grace and a littering of broken shell which gave them quite a crunch. Nonetheless, they wolfed it down and were soon on their way. I think both parties were more than glad to see the back of each other, however our intrepid travellers would never forget Wulf vis a vee!

Utter rubbish

W hen the bike was complete it looked fantastic, but the trouble was, as a racing motorcycle it was hopeless. Clive crashed the living daylights out of himself at every Grand Prix, and often during practice and qualifying. This was a big problem as the bike was usually rendered unrideable and our £200 start money was only paid to us if we took part in the race. Fortunately a couple of fellow competitors generously lent us their spare machines (yes, we were competing against teams that were so well backed they had complete spare bikes) so Clive could carry out what were termed 'start money specials' of just one lap duration. As this went on we were getting more and more skint. When I look back I do not know how on earth we survived.

The first event of the 1979 125cc Grand Prix series was at the Spanish GP, held once again at Jarama. This was the circuit where we had done so encouragingly well the previous year, but everything was in compete contrast this time as a big practice crash left the bike almost totally trashed. For no reason at all that he could fathom, Clive went down heavily at the fast uphill left-hander behind the paddock. He said: 'As soon as I asked something from the bike...Bang! down I went.'

We were so desperate for money that to save cash, Trevor and Clive had gone by themselves to Spain, and were using the tent for accommodation and as a workshop. This kept expenses and overheads to a bare minimum, and the two hundred quid start money was essential to our financial plan. But now, with an irreparable bike, they were in deep doo-doo. But up stepped Hans Muller, a rival who Clive had beaten on a number of occasions the previous year. Hans promptly offered his spare bike so we could pull off a start money special and keep our show on the road. What a wonderful group of people this daft sport so often attracts.

Tom Herron, who had softened towards us since our earlier frosty encounter, had by now risen to the heights of factory rider with Suzuki GB, and had become a father of twins. Clive's performances had earned the Irishman's respect, and the feeling was mutual. Tom had to fly home to Belfast immediately after the race to prepare for a big event in his home country, the NorthWest 200. This left his wife Andrea to drive home with their caravan and their young children, although she had the companionship of a girlfriend to help wrangle the twins. Clive and Trevor too were enlisted to assist. As they were driving back to the UK by road, would they mind accompanying Andrea's party to Santander, where they were to catch the ferry, just in case any blokeish support was needed en route? It was quite a distance, and over the Pyrenees.

As it happened Andrea reached the ferry port without incident, but at the ticket office she found she didn't have enough Spanish cash for the fare. It is a hellishly expensive, twenty-four hour crossing. Clive volunteered his meagre start money to help. No bother, she could pay him back at our next meeting, the Isle of Man TT. Tom would see us right over there, and apart from being honourable people, there was no question they were good for it. Tom was on monster start money that year.

But Tom never made it to the TT. He was killed in Ireland competing in the NorthWest 200. Road racing is indeed a cruel sport. On the whole it is full of wonderful, supportive, generous, lovely people who certainly do not deserve to die as punishment for making a small mistake. Sadly, that is what often happens. Our dire pecuniary circumstances were further reduced as a result of this latest tragic loss in our midst, but of course it was absolutely nothing compared to the terrible pain suffered by Andrea and the twins.

In the Isle of Man Clive decided that year's TT would be his last. Having returned to the pits during practice after riding Robin's 250 Yamaha around at a disappointingly low average speed, he simply said: 'I don't want to die any more'. An average lap speed on a 250 cc bike of 100 mph had become the yardstick, absolutely de rigueur, for anyone who wanted to be taken seriously in the class, and he had been slower than that. I asked him why he was so off the pace, and I was a bit cross, to be honest, as we had all made such a big effort just to be there. That was when he said he no longer wanted to die. Maybe it was Tom's demise that tipped him over the edge, I don't know. It was not something that had ever concerned him in that way before. I was relieved a little later when it sank in. Thank God he no longer wants to die! And for us that was the end of our romance with the Isle of Man. For ever.

We travelled to the Yugoslavian GP directly after the TT, travelling in our truck, towing our caravan, and carrying a bike with no cylinders on it. But no worries, it was all planned out. Some weeks before this the barrels had been given to Clive's new friend Hans Muller. Hans had then delivered them to a firm in Stuttgart where they were to be re-plated with a special coating called Nikasil. By now they would be on their way to Yugoslavia where we would be reunited with them ready for us to use at the Grand Prix at Rijeka.

We were almost totally broke but there was another two hundred quid start money to collect after the race, and we had a cunning plan to save money travelling to Yugoslavia. We would go through Belgium, Germany, Switzerland, Italy and Austria. A long trip, but this way we avoided the horrendous tolls payable on the French Autoroutes. Then we would reach our destination via the

Klagenfurt Pass, this being a route Trevor had taken a few years previously when he went camping with some friends.

The further we travelled, the more our meagre funds thinned, but we made it to the beginning of the Klaggenfurt where we started seeing signs saying Sens Interdit and Sens Verboten accompanied by a picture of a lorry with a trailer and a red line through it. It's alright, we reasoned, it doesn't apply to us. We're not in a lorry. We are driving a truck with a caravan. A few kilometres later there were more signs, only this time the picture was of a car and a caravan with the dreaded red line through it. We were all right though, we reckoned, we are not in a car, we are driving a truck with a caravan, and anyway, apart from that, we have a first gear of such a low ratio it will pull us up a sheer cliff face.

The road gradually got steeper - seven percent, then 11 percent, then 15 then 18. Ooh Lordy, that was a toughy! Then another stretch at 18 percent which we approached from a tight hairpin bend, that was an absolute mother. The truck coped, and we kept going, albeit slowly. Then we were passed by a kid on a moped with his girlfriend on the back. He was zigzagging up the road in a slalom-like fashion, trying to take the sting out of the steepness. The next sign we saw announced that a 21 percent gradient was coming up immediately after the next hairpin. The truck's poor engine was groaning and moaning like a ship's mast in a gale but still we kept going. We must have made about 200 metres up this killer, but then the truck just stopped. The poor thing could not go on against this beast.

What were we to do? It was so narrow we couldn't turn around, and there was no way we could carry on up. While we were scratching our heads an Austrian arrived in a Range Rover and offered to tow the caravan up for one thousand Austrian schillings. Presumably it was how he made his living. We counted up and all we had was £11 in cash and a ¾ full tank of diesel, every drop of which which we needed to get the rest of the way to Rijeka. And somehow we had to eat, so the would-be rescuer was waved away. By now Mr Clive 'no worries, we will fix it' Horton was for once completely devoid of ideas, to the point of knuckle biting.

Trevor took charge. Cometh the hour, cometh the man! 'Right,' said Trev, 'We unhitch the caravan, turn it round by hand, then jiggle the truck through 180 degrees, re-hitch and get on our way via some other route.' I could see Clive had grave doubts. By now it was night, we were on a 21 percent slope with a sheer cliff wall on one side and a huge drop on the other shielded only by an Armco barrier. But devoid of a better plan he kept quiet. I just sat in the truck with my arms around the children thinking, that's it, it's all over, good-bye caravan (I could envisage our prized asset plunging headlong into the black void below - it was a very dark night). It's been a crap year, I thought, let's all go home.

I heard the caravan being unhitched, then a BANG! when the emergency brake was snatched on as the retaining wire broke. The brakes worked though, and Clive threw himself between the caravan and the Armco to prevent it getting damaged. He wasn't suicidal you understand, he did it to protect our most valuable possession. Somehow they managed to turn the caravan around without injury or death, at which point the kid on the moped appeared once again, only this time without his other half. 'Hast du seen mien freunden gisehen?' The gradient had proved too much even for the slaloming bike, and the girl had got off to walk while the boy cajoled the thing to the summit. Where she had got to we knew not. Were they ever reunited? I hope so.

We eased our way down and set about finding a more manageable route. Trevor could not understand why we had been beaten back. 'I don't remember it being so steep. My mates and I had absolutely no problem when we took that route.' Later he let out that he had been on a GL1000 Honda Gold Wing. Quite frankly, it would have taken a tank trap to stop one of those battlecruisers. No wonder he couldn't remember having a problem! Anyway, it all goes to show you can't overcome Sens Interdit signs armed only with a positive mental attitude. You also need a Range Rover, or a Honda Gold Wing.

When we finally arrived at the circuit and were pitching up we came into contact with some of the locals, and they were decidedly different to other Europeans we had come across. Their sticker-begging habits were like something from the Third World. All the local school children collected stickers from race teams. 'Stickers, stickers!' they clamoured, holding out their grubby hands and affecting a pathetic look intended to appear waif-like, downtrodden and soulful, but which in fact made them look like idiotic bad actors.

We had a rival in another team who had his own unique way of dealing with these 'fans'. He would teach them English. Quite how he felt qualified for this task beats me, as he was an Australian, but nevertheless he would insist they say, 'Excuse me, may I have some stickers please?' When they had been sufficiently drilled to have got this off pat, he would then reply: " NO! Now bugger off!'

One of the good things about eastern European countries like Yugoslavia was our £11 budget lasted well when it came to buying provisions. The thing was, though, we had travelled all this way with the Red Menace, as I had come to call our bike, with no cylinders attached to its engine, and now we had a real disaster on our hands. When our German friend had called in to collect them in Stuttgart they were not finished, and he arrived at Rijeka empty-handed. Aaaaagh!

We were now very deeply in the mire. We were in the arsehole of Europe with less than £11 in 'our pockets and now we had no prospect of collecting the start money we needed to escape. I think you can guess where this might be going. Yes, up popped another Good Samaritan, this time in the form of Bruno Kneubuhler, a Swiss ex-gymnast turned motorcycle racer (his doctor had advised him to give up gymnastics as it was too dangerous. True!). Bruno became a very good racer indeed and, of course, being a proper European he did it in a more professional manner than your average Brit. We prefer to see our sporting heroes getting by on boyish charm, self-motivation, enthusiastic amateurism and other such dopy virtues. In contrast the European sportsman adopts a napoleonic attitude and goes armed to win. We do, however, milk our amateurishness unashamedly, or at least our media does, whenever we have our occasional small successes.

Our kind Swiss friend lent Clive a full set of cylinders, cylinder heads and pistons - the best part of half an engine - not just so we could complete a lap and claim our start money, but to actually compete in the race. What a guy. If in his declining years he is ever in need of a kidney, Clive will give him one of his. It would be the least he could do.

We got out of Yugoslavia alive and clutching our hard-earned start money. The race performance was nothing to write home about. I can't even remember what happened. This was a very sorry period in our racing lives, and it was not yet even at its lowest point. That would come a little later! Next up, Team Horton took part in the Dutch TT, where another valuable lesson was learned about the importance of good race preparation. Not a lesson concerning mechanical preparedness for the wonderful Trevor, but a problem in the rider's head. A journalist friend had lent Clive a book he highly recommended entitled Marathon Man. Clive took advantage of every spare moment to read it, and he engineered many such moments during the Dutch TT weekend. Trevor dutifully worked on the bike, I did everything else, and he just read the damned book, right up to departing the caravan for the race.

The standard Morbidelli that was used in 1978. A better bike than the "world beater" designed by Clive for 1979, which was never quite as it should have been

Clive sat in his leather suit and boots, reading away while Trevor warmed up the bike. Then, with just minutes to go, we somehow prised it out of his fingers and managed to lever him off the caravan seat and onto the bike, whereupon he went out on the track and rode like a complete nonentity, finishing 14th. No surprise really following such a switched off mental build up. Where was the pre-race anticipation, the nerves, the surge of adrenalin? There was none of this, and therefore not much of a result. To be fair, the bike was later found to have a damaged piston, so maybe he could have done a little better if the bike had been fully on song, but he didn't deserve a good result that day anyway.

A nasty taste

We journeyed the short distance to the Belgian GP which would take place for the first time on a shortened version of the Spa Francorchamps circuit, reduced to four miles in length from the traditional layout's nine. This involved massive earthworks and civil engineering and the project had been going on for the past 12 months. In part it entailed cutting a huge swathe down a steep hillside and through an Ardennes pine forest for a new section of track and sufficient run off areas, and then asphalting the race surface.

When we arrived the work had almost been completed but, shock, horror, the paddock wasn't finished and we had to camp in a field while they laid a tarmac surface for us to park on. In fact, the race surface itself was still being laid! There was supposed to be a Grand Prix starting in three days, how on earth was that going to happen?

Well, I'll tell you. In order for the surface to be laid as quickly and smoothly as possible, the navvies (or whatever they are called in Belgium) added diesel to the mix. Yes, I know what you are thinking. A racing surface with diesel in it! Clearly those clowns did not have a brain among them. Quite astonishing.

Eventually, very slowly, teams began moving into the paddock following the tarmac laying vehicle and the roller, and we selected our parking spot next door to the reigning 250cc world champion Kork Ballington. The surface was still steaming hot as it hadn't gone off yet, making us hop about a bit and almost melting one's shoes. Whatever, we got set up, as did Kork. But as soon as we were sorted out we were approached by a twit wearing an armband.

You know the sort, During the week he is simply 'Jules Savon' but give him an armband and suddenly he is a somebody. He is transmogrified into the highly important person he always knew he was. This chap puffed his chest out and in his very best Belgian-English told us we would have to up sticks and move because this area had been reserved for the technical control department. Clive explained to him in no uncertain terms that as he had had a year in which to sort this out, it was not acceptable for him to come along now and retrospectively bag the spot. 'Sorry mate, no can do. You are too late. It will take an hour to reload and the only remaining places left for us to park instead are distant mud holes. So, no chance pal.' Kork backed us all the way and also told him he would have to site the technical area somewhere else.

Monsieur Armband went away, very fromaged off indeed, returning five minutes later to play his ace card. This was a deadly weapon often used against racing types to devastating effect, one that strikes at their very being. To understand this, it is important to realise racers live to race. They need it so badly they are like drug addicts overdue their next hit. You have to imagine, as a drug addict, your dealer turning up and saying, 'Right, move your car or you get no dope, man.' Imagine you need to score so badly you're shaking with withdrawal symptoms. You're going to move aren't you? That's what Monsieur Brassard (French for armband) was banking on when he announced: 'No move - NO START!' 'Sod it then,' said Clive and Kork in unison, we won't start.

The official was dumbfounded. This had never happened to him before. He'd gone nuclear and it had no effect. His world had turned upside down. He stomped off, never to return, and the tech people based themselves somewhere else. Furthermore the two teams kept their starts and earned themselves a good deal of self respect. Kork, of course, was a big hitter at the time, but it was pretty brave of us nevertheless, as we were, as usual, desperate for the start money.

I liked Kork Ballington. Clive always thought he could beat him but I don't think he ever did. He was calm, level-headed, and champion of the world, but also a really nice guy and not a bighead or a show off. He had a massive moustache, but not a massive ego. There was a bit of David Niven about him. A gentleman. Unlike some riders I could mention, he would never get hammered and start falling about and spewing up and have to be carried back to the van to sleep it off!

Clive with Keith Huewen. Another GP regular at the time

Clive particularly respected the South African privateer Jon Ekerold. Jon was a hard man and he once said he'd ride over a rival to win if he had to, but that was just him getting inside somebody's head. He was just a regular guy travelling from race to race with a wife and a couple of kids, a set up very similar to ours in many ways, but he was another champion of the world. Clive really admired him, and I can see why, but he was not entirely my kind of guy.

Having said that, Jon and his family would always talk to us. It's interesting. Looking back now the riders I didn't mind him being on the track with tended to be well mannered and polite off it as well. There were some snooty people we'd see at every meeting and I'd think, we've been in the same paddock for so many years, why can't you just say hello?

Anyway, with all the hoo-hah about parking in the paddock the meeting had begun badly and things got progressively worse. The 50cc riders went out first for practice, setting off like a swarm of bees, and while they were out on track it started to rain a little, making the diesel-mix surface absolutely lethal. The 50cc guys were complaining about wheel spin! Practice was then abandoned while the organisers got contractors in to cut grooves into the tarmac rather like tyre treads, hoping it would offer some kind of grip.

The following day there was a riders' meeting. A petition was got up and a strike was called for. Most riders signed the petition including us, but we were aching for the start money. If we failed to start we wouldn't get a bean. The upshot was the strike took place and most of the top riders withdrew from the meeting, but the organisers would not buckle and insisted the races went ahead with depleted grids for full championship points. We decided we needed the money so badly we absolutely had to start.

On the eve of race day the spectators started to arrive, and when they heard the stars would not be performing they got a bit cheesed off to say the least. Not with the riders, but with the organisers, and some promptly commenced setting fire to the straw bales protecting the Armco barriers. Well, this caused something of a wild party atmosphere, with much jeering and carrying on, and the fire service was called in to deal with the situation.

At that time the men of the Belgian Fire Brigade, or Brandweer, weren't like our blokes, all uniformed and professional. No, they had long hair and looked like hooligans themselves. Their arrival prompted even more jeers as the crowd poked fun, and bent the hoses in half to stop the flow of water. In short, it turned into bedlam, and when we went to bed the noise and chaos was continuing, and it kept up for most of the night.

On race day, Clive was in a terrible dilemma. In his heart he wanted to back the strike, but we, his family, needed to eat. We had already, by this time, cut back to only eating on even numbers in the month. Just kidding! But things were almost that bad. Trevor prepared the bike and as Clive put his leathers on, he was approached by a good friend of ours, a journalist and a key propagator of the strike, Barry Coleman. Barry proceeded to lay into Clive, putting him under huge moral and emotional pressure. It was quite unbelievable, and simply the worst possible mental preparation anyone could envisage for someone about to be sent out to race a motorcycle (even worse than reading Marathon man!). Incidentally, it was Barry who had given Clive that very book!

Our poor rider was a wreck and he went to the start line crying, I'd never seen him like it, ever. What a mess. Anyway, the upshot was he compromised and did yet another start money special. This satisfied both camps to a degree, but himself not at all. A bit of prize money, would have been very handy and it was well within his reach that day. All in all it was a miserable affair, and one rider, was left with such an unpleasant taste in his mouth he retired from the sport. Trevor never spoke to the journalist again.

A bit of a turnaround

I n the middle of the season at Donington Park, Clive had a
chance conversation with well-known motorcycle engineer Ron
Williams of Maxton Engineering. Ron was the go-to man if you had
handling problems. So much so, even Honda consulted him! Clive
described the problems he was experiencing, and Ron looked over
the heart-breaking bike, suggesting afterwards it needed to be three
inches shorter. That seemed a bit drastic, so we compromised on
two, and Spondon Engineering made us a shorter swinging arm.
What a difference! A test session at Mallory Park was all it took to
realise the changes had turned the Red Menace into a competitive
bike. The improvement was so marked, we wondered why on earth
we hadn't worked it out for ourselves.

The next two grands prix were in Sweden and Finland. Clive joined
up with Chas Mortimer's team again hitching his van to our
caravan, and this time both Trevor and I were left at home. We
couldn't complain as we were only too aware we were living on a
pecuniary knife edge. On the subject of tight finances, Chas
reckoned he had discovered a new and much cheaper way to get his
bikes to Sweden. His plan was that while he made his way separately
by car, his Australian mechanic Lionel Angel, and Aussie rider
Barry Smith would take the van through East Germany to catch a
ferry across the Baltic from Rostock to Helsingborg. By cutting out
Denmark, this avoided two expensive ferries. While not as broke as
we were, Chas was always keen to save a few quid.

The East German roads were a bit rough to say the least. Not much
traffic on them, but bouncier than Tigger who is known to be quite
a wonderful bouncer. After a while Clive and the Aussies pulled
over, opened up the caravan and set about making themselves a cup
of tea and a bite to eat. A few minutes later there was heavy banging

on the door and upon opening it there was revealed the stern face of a Stasi stormtrooper, a member of the East German Secret Police. This chap then played his part like a stereotype in a movie, demanding: 'Papers, you show me papers!' The chaps proffered their transit visa which caused the Stasi man great consternation, as it did not allow for any sort of stop!

'Achtung! You must move on immediately!' said the scary policeman. But he was dealing with two Australians and an anti-establishment Englishman who politely told him they would indeed move on, but not until they had finished their lunch, had a cup of tea and completed a game of cricket! He cleared off, twitching. I don't think he had been spoken to quite like that before.

The lunch break was not the only time they spent parked up in East Germany. Later on they hid away and spent the night behind the iron curtain in the country as the ferry wasn't booked until the following day. Unsurprisingly, when they arrived at the border checkpoint all hell broke loose. 'Vy hat ist so lange commen zu hier? 'We spent the night.' 'Vot is dast?? Die nacht verbringen! Ein transitvisum? Das ist verboten!' 'OK sorry, we won't do it again.' 'Blutige holle. Making all time sure nicht!' With that, a guard was sent into the back of the van to poke about in the straw with a bayonet. Actually, there was no straw, but you get what I mean.

Clive finished sixth in Sweden, surviving a severe scorching to his nether regions caused by the tyre having worn through the fibreglass seat due to it having been moved forward by the shorter swinging arm. In Finland he was tenth.

At some time during these adventures in northern Europe, Clive had to get something out of the caravan, and when he was inside the Aussies thought it would be a bit of a laugh to drive off with him in it. This was a new experience, as he had never travelled inside it before. All was well at first, but as the rig gathered speed he was alarmed to discover, the caravan's fixtures wobbling around like crazy - cupboards and beds almost floating free! What the heck was going on? Later it became clear: the A-frame of the chassis, had broken and the caravan body had become partially detached. Oh my! Now the caravan, our major asset, was falling apart.

Clive press-ganged a German welder to join the frame back together again, and I knew nothing of this disaster until the boys returned to England. The money saved by going on those terrible East German roads was all lost on the caravan. Ah well, that's life! Upon Clive's return we travelled to Northamptonshire once again to the British Grand Prix at Silverstone. This time, however, there was no fairytale result. Clive finished tenth and that was our last finish of the season. All in all our world-beating bike had been a big disappointment. Clive remembers being passed down the straight at Silverstone by a standard 35bhp Morbidelli ridden by Stefan Dorflinger; a chap who usually finished behind him. Worse, it was Stefan's 'spare ride', as he was concentrating on the 50cc class that year, and paying little heed to the development needs of his 125. So much for Harald's 40bhp!

Clive was exhausted, demoralised, and mentally down and out, so with six weeks of the domestic season left, he quit, packed it all in, and stopped racing. 'I've finished with it', he said, 'I've had enough.' We concentrated fully on home life, and Trevor and Leigh opened a motorcycle shop together.

Far from being a serious attack on the world championships, the 1979 season had been a humiliating disaster, both financially crippling and a massive set back in all mental departments. All the things that keep a racer's brain in gear took a heavy beating - self confidence, self esteem, self belief, self respect. OK, there are rather a lot of selfs in there, but these inner reserves are the only fuel riders have to draw on. If his sense of humour had not still been functioning I would have diagnosed clinical depression, it was that bad.

Anyway, that was it, or so we thought. We worked on the house, we bought a carpet for the lounge, and we were given a PVC suite by a relative so we finally had some soft seats and we started using the sitting room for the first time in four years. Clive even installed some new window frames, and we started to behave like a conventional family.

Clive would sometimes take Daniel to the park to kick a ball or play on the swings. During one of these sessions he noticed that the slide didn't work too well. It was stainless steel alright, but dull, weathered, and a bit sticky. So the next time they went to the park he took some Mr Sheen polish and applied it, and Dan and his fellow sliders polished it to a fine shine with their backsides and the slide got faster and faster. It wasn't long before the kids were zooming down at record speeds and flying off the end like Evel Knievel. The children were airborne for two meters or more before landing heavily on the concrete playground and it finally occurred to Clive it might be a good idea to take the can of Mr Sheen and depart the scene. He shoved Daniel under one arm and discreetly left the park.

Supposedly, our racing days were over, but when we got into October and entries were invited for the 'Race of The South' at Brands Hatch, which was the last international event of the year, Clive decided we would enter on the 250 Yamaha, just to see how it went. It went very well. He finished second in his heat and in the top ten in the 250cc final. This meant, of course, we would try one more year as a professional racing team. I am told it often takes several attempts to get off heroin, and it is my belief racing bikes is a drug that is even more addictive.

Cotton Socks

T he 1980s started very humbly indeed. We sold the 125cc race bike, the patched-up caravan and the long-suffering Transit, replacing the last of these with a four litre 3.5 ton Fiat panel van, planning to convert it into a motor home cum transporter cum workshop. Robin's Yamahas were sold as he had another, more pressing interest - spending time with his newborn son.

So we could all still eat, Clive was working part-time for a motorcycle dealer in Nottingham, and trying to drum up support for another season on the tracks. He signed a contract with Kangol Helmets, travelling 200 miles up to Stranraer in a borrowed car to seal the deal, but at that time he did not have any motorcycles to ride. But a few weeks later, out of the blue, up stepped local businessman Dave Orton with an offer of machinery.

Dave was a well-known sponsor of motorcycle racing, and his Appleby Glade business empire was based only 12 miles from our home, so the enterprise had a very tidy feel to it. He remembered Clive from the 125 race in the first ever British GP at Silverstone in 1977, saying he had been right royally entertained by his cornering antics on the Brader Brothers Maico. Thank goodness for people like Dave. Actually, I suspect John Cooper had a hand in this welcome turn of events. We always kept in touch with John and often visited him for his sage advice. He was well aware of our position.

Meanwhile, Ken Foster, the supplier of Clive's bike for the 125 Honda series, and sometime supporter of the Red Menace project, said he needed a fresh rider for his bike for the 1980 season. This meant we needed to find a new Honda dealer to maintain our place in this domestic championship which we had won three years before. We couldn't blame Ken for wanting a rider who would give the Honda series his full attention. We had been neglecting it for too long while following Clive's dream of becoming a world champion. A dream that we should have seen was doomed from the beginning, if only more logic had been applied instead of romantic wishful thinking.

A sad footnote to the Fosters of Chorlton chapter of our lives concerns Ken's mechanic, Ian, who worked at his dealership and looked after our Honda 125 in his spare time, doing an outstanding job. He committed suicide a few years later - rejection from a girl, I understand, was the catalyst. He was perhaps a slightly odd fellow, but we liked him and he was a good man. As Clive says, men usually take rejection pretty badly, and in some cases, devastatingly so.

One evening we were invited round to Dave Orton's lovely home to meet his family and talk about plans for the new season. He was incredibly supportive, and his friendly wife Diane was also delightful in her full support for Dave and his eccentric ideas about involvement in motorcycle racing.

We established Clive would ride a 250cc Cotton, a British-made bike which used a new Austrian Rotax engine as its power unit. Cotton was a new manufacturer on the scene but we thought it looked worth a gamble. A TZ350 Yamaha was also to be supplied, and Dave was keen for it to be a Maxton. Maxton Engineering was a top quality small volume manufacturer of special frames and suspension systems and, coincidentally, it was run by Ron Williams, the chap who issued the jolly good '…shorten it by three inches' advice during the disastrous 1979 season.

Clive said he would like to remain a professional racer rather than take a day job, which meant we needed one hundred and fifty pounds a week to live on, which in turn meant we would need to win twice that amount per week as we had to split our prize and start money 50/50 with Dave. Not a bad deal as Dave was supplying the bikes and covering all the running costs. Three hundred quid a week seemed a massive ask, but Dave's opinion was, 'I think you can do it!' It was a great feeling to be on the receiving end of so much faith in Clive's ability and of our joint determination. And as it turned out, Dave was bang on, and then some!

Dave asked me what vehicle I was driving at time. When I told him I was using our four litre 3.5 ton Fiat truck, he was appalled. 'We can't have you travelling to Sainsbury's in that!' he said, and without further ado he immediately fixed me up with the most delightful 1275cc white Mini Cooper, liberally decorated with fruit machine artwork. That was what Dave's business was all about - leasing one armed bandits and the new electronic tennis and space invader games that were everywhere in pubs in those days. I loved that little car, and I really felt like a 'somebody' when I was driving it, courting much attention and advertising Dave's business as I went about my daily chores.

Dave also signed up John Newbold, a butcher's son from Jacksdale, Nottingham, to ride in the 500cc class. Dave considered John to be the only bloke who, 'on his day', had the beating of Barry Sheene. Dave invited Clive and John over for lunch one day and took them out and got them blind, staggering drunk! Then, rather incongruously, he signed them both up as members of a gym called Tony Ford's Health Club. What was that all about? Dave knew exactly what he was doing. Clive went along to this gym three times a week from then on, and for a while he became a properly dedicated athlete and fitness freak.

1971 - Early days with the Bantam at Cadwell and Snetterton

A year on and in 1972 the fashion changed nearly as quickly as the machinery.

Though Clive was never much of a dresser

TT 1973. 7th place out of over 40 starters on his debut wasn't bad.

Note also the new 'corporate" livery. Team Horton were getting professional

1974 - The sweet handling Benelli (above) ***could only make 17th in the Production Race, but in the Lightweight*** (below) ***it was victory!***

*The podium, the photos, the Trophy
and all ready to go on and become
World Champion.........*

(Above) *On the new Robin Mayne Yamaha '75. Possibly the best result of the TT win. Another winner was the MBA in '78* (46 below). *Clive was 1ˢᵗ at Hengelo, Holland, Easter in the rain*

The French GP 1977 (above) ***and Mallory Park's Devil's Elbow***
1980 (below). ***It didn't always go to plan***

(Above and right) *The Foster's MT 125 Honda was a lot of fun in 1977 with the series proving hugely popular, Clive winning and the series being financially significant for us in subsequent years too.*

(Below and right) *The GP bikes could prove more of a handful, as captured by a photographer from one of the Italian magazines*

130

(Top left and above) *Our bikes were always well turned out and sometimes even up to date. Clive with discs and Astralite wheels, while others were still struggling with drum brakes.*

(Left) *The pretty MBA special of 1979 that became the "Red Menace"*

The ABC Honda provided us with plenty of wins. Though it is hard to imagine a one-make 125 series attracting GP stars today

(Top) *Riding for Appleby Glade* (Below Left) *The pretty MBA* (below Right) *Super mechanic Bill Bristow wearing his Randle Armstrong works overalls 1981*

A photo-call for Randle Racing. Clive always did his part when it came to publicity and promotion. Ultimately there just proved too little interest in the smaller classes, in the UK

The Randle Racing machines always looked the part. Good enough indeed to attract ex-350 World Champion Takazumi Katayama (below right) *to have a shufti at Daytona*

Beautiful machines for racing (above) *and posing* (below). *That film work was a bone of contention*

Clive and Noddy, as John was affectionally known, hit it off big time, both having a daft sense of humour. Noddy was a really funny guy and Clive liked him a lot. He was always prepared to see the funny side of a situation and never seemed to take life too seriously. You will notice I am referring to John in the past tense, as he was yet another rider who would be killed in action. John died at the NorthWest 200 in Northern Ireland two years later in 1982.

Another pair of nutters Dave Orton signed up for the 1980 season was sidecar crew Roger Dixon and his passenger Paul Appleby from Derby. Roger was a character and a half, well and truly rooted in the 1950s Teddy Boy era. He could sing a bit too! But how it was possible for a man to sound so good when he smoked, swore and drank like a frontline infantry man I have no idea. He particularly liked performing Guy Mitchell songs, 'Singing the Blues' being the most famous, of course. With this band of merry men Dave had just about every event covered on a typical British race weekend.

For the Honda MT125 championship Clive signed up to ride for a dealership called ABC Honda. Clive Wall, the manager of ABC, had known us for years, ever since our club racing days. He used to race himself on heavy British bikes such as 650cc BSAs and 750cc Norton Commandos, and occasionally he and our Clive, on his smaller, slower, lighter bikes, would clash on the track; sometimes in open practice, and once in a 500 mile race at Thruxton.

The Thruxton 500 was open to production road bikes, from 350cc to 750cc, so Clive used the 250cc Benelli he had raced at the TT and lied about its capacity on the entry form. During the long race he harassed bigger bikes constantly on his underpowered bike and Clive Wall, who had been competing on one of his big 750s, now remembered my Clive as a tiger. It might equally have been as an irritating little s**t, of course, but anyway he wanted him on his 125cc ABC Honda.

Clive Wall was a really professional guy. On one occasion we had a problem with the hydraulic front brake and we decided it needed a new set of seals, but boss Clive simply said: 'Just buy a complete new unit, don't mess around.' The difference in price was about £100, a lot of money at the time. No wonder he was a successful business manager. Don't mess about? Ha! My Clive would have been fiddling about for hours fitting seals to try to save money.

Clive acting the tart on my Dave Orton Mini. I loved it

I am hoping that by now you are absorbing the coincidences rather than being confused by them. Horton and Orton, Paul Appleby and Appleby Glade. All good fun, even if only for reasons of rhyming and alliteration. As for there being two Clives: it occurs to me that in fiction Clive is a name usually chosen for moustache-stroking Dick Dastardly-type characters.

Stove-ja-vu

O ur big Fiat van had a sliding door on one side giving access to an area that we converted into motorhome-esque facilities featuring two bunk beds and a couple of cupboards. It was even carpeted! Sidecar passenger Paul Appleby was a carpet fitter in the week and he did a great job of it. Despite these luxuries, having sold the caravan we were taking a bit of a step backwards in terms of trackside living conditions. Never mind, thanks to Dave and Clive at least we were moving forwards on the track!

We were not quite back to Viva van standards, but not that far away. At least I could stand up to use the two ring gas burner in the Fiat as it was mounted on one of the cupboards. Unfortunately I have no photographs of all this as I didn't see the need for memory-jogging mental stimulation down the line. Actually, I have to admit we were pretty poor at taking photographs altogether. We were always focused on the present and in shaping the immediate future rather than bothering to collect memories as we went along, and that is something we do regret a little now.

The Fiat featured a divider that closed the driver's cab off from the rear of the vehicle, and in this panel there was a sliding access door so we could reach the poor children travelling behind in the 'motor home'. There were no seats or seat belts back there, of course. We would just chuck 'em in the back and hope they went to sleep on the bunks. Daniel, at this time, had a huge plastic flute, and when we were driving along one day he was tooting away on it while marching fore and aft in the rear. Then there was an emergency of some sort and we stopped rather suddenly, and the flute was rammed down his throat. What a mess, and there were buckets of tears, but he lived. It seems to me, if a child can survive parenting like this, he will be toughened up to the extent it greatly increases his chances of making it successfully through the rest of his life.

The racing went well from the start of the season, although it turned out the Cotton concern was more than a little strapped for cash. Such a typically British state of affairs. We seem to struggle to get beyond a make do and mend, wartime-type philosophy and psychology. The machines were sold via Honda dealer Bill Smith's Manchester motorcycle empire, but the struggling northern factory seemed a good match for our struggling little team. We had much in common. The relationship was tested, however, when Dave was sent a bill for services that were at best only 'moderately rendered'.

Early on in the season Clive had a big dice with Charlie Williams at Mallory Park. Charlie was at this time a semi-works Yamaha rider, and he was on the latest factory product. In the qualifying race, Clive broke the lap record, but the following day, in the final Charlie won the race and broke it once again. Clive decided to give Charlie best in this race as he was not confident in the Cotton's handling. He thought, 'Sod it Charlie, the race is yours, I'll come home second this time.' The thought was hardly formed when Bang! down he went at a corner called Devil's Elbow. The bike was smashed up and Clive was shaken, but more than anything he was angry about the injustice of the situation. 'I'd given it up,' said Clive. 'I was happy to cruise home in second. God is indeed a b*****d!' We subsequently found out the bike's front suspension was a cheap, unsophisticated road bike unit, and totally unsuitable for the job.

The crash brought about a problem. The bike needed fixing for a race at Oulton Park in Cheshire the following day. The Cotton factory boss suggested our mechanics, Trevor (who was back with us for this weekend) and our friend Bill Bristow (a refugee from the Fosters Honda days), could use the factory workshop facilities to repair it overnight. As Cotton's premises were in Manchester, and not too far from Oulton, we decided to give it a go.

Bill and Trevor are massive characters, and without them we would never have survived on so many occasions. Sure enough, they rose to the challenge magnificently, and despite lack of sleep and there being no financial incentive whatsoever, they turned up on time at Oulton Park where the bike performed beautifully, leaving everyone brimming with optimism for the rest of the season. Clive probably finished second to Charlie again, it is so long ago, I can't remember. Who knows or cares!

Anyway, a couple of days later Dave received an invoice from Cotton for the repairs! Clive was in his office at the time and Dave was apparently incredulous. He telephoned the Cotton CEO and gave him a right mouthful, telling him to shove his invoice where the sun shines the least. No more was heard of it. You didn't mess with Dave Orton let me tell you!

Another incident which needs an airing took place at Mallory Park once again. Getting ready for the first round of the Honda 125 Championship, we had sent off for entry forms and applied for some start money. We were a professional outfit and had had starting money before, and we thought we should receive some again. Starting or, rather, appearance money was always a bit of a grubby business. Some riders got huge amounts while others had to pay to enter the same races. All we wanted was a free entry and a bit of financial recognition.

The secretary in charge gave us a free entry, but said although we may have been a professional team, he didn't see why he should pay us any starting money. We immediately placed him on our 'no Christmas card' list! Whatever, we had little choice but to accept the decision. We needed the prize money, and we were obligated to Appleby Glade and to ABC.

The Leathers say ABC but Clive is actually on the 350cc Randle Yamaha. Sometimes we were so busy between races there was no time to change "costume". He's back of the pack, but not for long

Clive decided that although we would race, we would implement a work to rule (there was no riders' trade union of course, it was just for us as individuals). The idea was that apart from Clive's efforts on the track, we would just do the minimum we could get away with. Ideally, this boiled down to him wining the 125cc race, but not taking part in a lap of honour or attending the rostrum and prize-giving ceremonies. Officials love that kind of stuff. It makes them look like benefactors and part of the establishment as they dole out the cups and stand by proudly in their crested blazers.

Before the 125 race I could see Clive was tense and nervous. Fully suited up, he was pacing up and down the paddock, well in the mood for a race and super-determined to win. Pacing, pacing, pacing. Sure enough, he won the race in fine style after a good scrap with other riders. Now he was determined to knee the secretary of the meeting in the groin, metaphorically speaking, and to expose him as the cretin we thought he was. Post race, Clive got changed as quickly as he possibly could and ignored all calls to go to the rostrum. Messengers who came to find him were sent back with the answer: 'No, I'm working to rule!' The big boss from Honda UK duly appeared and royally bollocked him for making the ceremony look daft, and for denying ABC the publicity exposure they deserved. He said he had no sympathy with our position and stomped off.

Shortly after the the brouhaha had died down, a man we had never met before, approached us in the paddock and introduced himself as one of ABC's directors. Oh-oh! we thought. This could mean the sack. But no, he simply said: 'I just want you to know you have my full support for your 'principled position.' Well, what a result.

The biggest prize in our sights that season was the Vladivar Vodka 250cc British Championship. We did very well all told, despite a dodgy decision at one round whereby Clive was given third instead of second in a photo finish. No electronics were used in those days, and unlike in horse racing, no photographs either - it was all down to the judgement of myopic timekeepers. Furthermore, there was no procedure or facility for protesting a result. We just had to take it on the chin. And at another round, in a wet and miserable race at Snetterton, Clive rode like a complete twit, his Rain God status having by then been long left behind in the bottom of a muddy Flanders dyke.

Keep calm and carry on

We squeezed in a few Grands Prix that season too, the Dutch TT at Assen being one. The Dutch always ran to a different timetable to most GPs. First practice was held on Wednesday evening, followed by sessions on Thursday and Friday, and the race was then run on the Saturday. In other countries racing took place on Sundays.

In the Wednesday evening session, Clive was fastest in the 250cc class, ahead of reigning world champion Anton Mang. When the British press hounds arrived the following day and reviewed the time sheets they were all delirious with excitement and rushed to see him, planning to write upbeat stories about an upset being on the cards. Clive put them right. 'It means nothing,' he told them. 'All it says is I had the right tyres on and most of the others didn't. It was damp and I had intermediates on, that was all. It was just luck so keep your knickers on.' It was not what they had wanted to hear and they trudged off with empty notebooks, looking somewhat forlorn and slump-shouldered.

Clive, on the other hand, was secretly quite encouraged. It rather went to his head if I'm honest, and as a result of his over enthusiasm in weakening the air-fuel mixture (for improved performance do you see? Fastest, is never enough for these ambitious lunatics) the bike kept seizing. I should explain that Clive was chief mechanic on that trip, with his younger brother David as an assistant. Now 16, and much grown up since getting himself lost at Assen four years previously, David did everything that was asked of him. He did a really good job, in fact, but someone with more experience such as Trevor or Bill would have had the know-how and authority to question an over-zealous superior officer.

Seizing is when, due to overheating or lack of lubrication, an engine suddenly stops, instantly locking the rear wheel. I like the Italian words for this: 'gripaggio' or 'gripato'. The grip part tells you all you need to know - the piston grips the cylinder wall suddenly, firmly and absolutely relentlessly. If you are quick in disengaging the clutch you save a crash, if not the rear wheel locks and a crash usually results. Clive was always very quick! A good job because in every Thursday and Friday qualifying session the bike seized solid, usually at a place called Post Seven, which was the furthest possible point on the track from the paddock. Worse, the seizure always occurred before he could get down to setting a fast lap time.

Clive's vanity cost three pistons and one wrecked cylinder and he qualified last on the grid only by virtue of his best time during Wednesday evening's session. That in itself had been a miracle; that he finally summoned the sense to set the bike up for Saturday's race, exactly as it had been on that first damp evening was another.

On race day brother David was assigned to operate the pit board on his own. I couldn't help as I was lap-scoring and baby-sitting from a position half-way round the lap and reached from the other side of the paddock. Most riders like to know their position in the race, how many laps are remaining, and how many seconds behind them the bloke behind them is. They can work everything else out by themselves.

The Dutch TT was quite a short race in terms of the number of laps as the circuit in those days was relatively long. After four laps Clive was in the top six and going like the clappers and David was accurately counting off the laps and doing a perfect job with the board. But then Clive sensed he could hear another engine close behind him so at the next turn he left his braking very late and hit the gas extra hard on the exit. He crashed! Guess which bend it was. Correct! Post Seven. Mad as hell with himself he jumped up quickly, pulled the bike straight and removed sods of grass, then restarted and set off once again. With his hair on fire! I could see on my watch he was 20 seconds late coming past me and I knew exactly what had occurred when I saw bits of grass and straw still attached to the bike.

David, meanwhile, never wavered and he continued to signal perfectly, giving Clive accurate information on every lap, and not being thrown despite knowing full well our rider had suddenly fallen behind schedule. You have to admire a young boy of that age maintaining such discipline. Due to his sterling efforts, with two laps to go Clive was able to work out that the group in sight up ahead were racing for seventh to tenth place, and that the gaggle included a rival on super-good machinery with super support, whom, it must be said carried a bit of a swagger.

Clive thought to himself that he would get among them before the race ended, and he did. He managed ninth, failing to catch his cocksure rival by a matter of inches. A good race, one of his best in fact. It's interesting, you don't have to win to have a good race. You just have to never give up, never give in, and make absolutely certain nothing whatever is left in the tin. When that happens, these are the best of racing days.

Oh Vienna

Traditionally, after the Dutch TT, the competitors would immediately make their way to Spa Francorchamps, traditional home of the Belgian Grand Prix, which was always run the following weekend. But in 1980, following the debacle there the previous year, the Belgian world championship round was scheduled to take place at Zolder, around 70km east of Antwerp. It had been hoped 12 months of weathering would wash the diesel out of the Spa track surface, but in the end the reconfigured Spa Francorchamps had been deemed unsafe and off we all went to Zolder, an unfamiliar circuit for most of us, and a surprisingly pleasant place it was too.

The weather was lovely and the facilities were first-class, and our stupendously fit rider continued his good form. And he was fit too. After six months training with Tony Ford, Clive had sculpted muscle definition, carried no excess weight and looked altogether marvellous and athletic. It didn't help him though, when during the last few laps of the race, while in a strong fourth place, he experienced for the first time in his career debilitating dehydration. He said: 'It comes on suddenly, affecting your brain so you find yourself fighting disorientation. How do I do this? How far do I lean the bike over? Something that was second nature moments ago is suddenly unfathomable. How hard do I need to squeeze the brakes?'

He was passed by two riders on those final laps and there was nothing he could do to put up a fight. His vision was impaired too, and when he climbed off the bike at the end, he was in a zombie-like state, literally foaming at the mouth. Not an attractive sight, frankly, but I knew he needed water. Although it could have been even better he was chuffed to be sixth, but being even dafter than usual.

A good drink of water and he recovered in just a few minutes, spitting out gobbets of something foul that did nothing to improve his diminished attractiveness. Another lesson learned at great expense: make sure you are correctly hydrated. Simply looking good isn't enough. A drink of water before the race and he may even have made the rostrum that day, who knows?

We also entered the German Grand Prix at the famous Nurburgring, high in the Eiffel mountains, and we drove there via the Rotax factory near Vienna, Austria, to have our engine rebuilt in the firm's 'tool shop'. Clive spent the best part of two days in the factory, while I did the gypsy thing with our two children in the works car park. We needed supplies, so I walked to the nearest shops with the children to buy provisions. It was a fair distance, to be honest - well, you don't get supermarkets near factories do you? No matter, we had time to spare anyway. Daniel was by then a robust four and Emma two and in a pushchair. It was something for us all to do, but we were battling somewhat during the return journey.

The pushchair was loaded to the gunwales and I had given Dan two heavy bags which, after a while, he just couldn't manage any longer. What to do? Daniel spotted some burly builders with a van and encouraged me to ask them for a lift. He was four and taking charge! They were so helpful and obliging, and really pleased to have met us. They had seen the van with its Appleby Glade logos parked in the Rotax car park and wondered who we were. We got a lift and their curiosity was satisfied!

It was another difficult couple of days for me to be honest, although the children thought all this was normal life and seemed to love it. The tool shop guys took Clive motocrossing after work. He didn't enjoy it I'm afraid, but he grinned and bore it. He can't do dirty motorbike stuff very well, and he is hopeless on trials bikes as well as the fast mud-plugging stuff. Never mind, the extra 500 miles we covered to call in on the Rotax factory was usually well worth it as the engine always performed better after a visit to its birthplace. Soon we were off on our first visit to the chilly Ring in the wet and foggy Eiffel mountains.

The Nurburgring is a truly magnificent circuit, reminiscent of the Isle of Man TT course in many ways. And as is the case on the Island, circuit knowledge is king. Each lap of the Ring is 13 miles, and with just four allocated practice periods per class, its secrets are impossible to unlock in one visit, especially as most track sessions take place in the rain or in inhospitably cold fog. Clive did report loving the carousels, as the specially banked corners were named. These were hairpin corners banked steeply in the bottoms and made from council paving slabs that were so viciously bumpy, hanging onto the handlebars felt like gripping the firing handles of a 50 calibre machine gun. A new experience is always welcomed if you are a racer or a drug addict, but altogether we were not expecting too much, and when he retired in the race due to water in the works, I suspect it was something of a relief.

We loaded up and set off to Oulton Park for a race the following day, which was August Bank Holiday Monday. It had all been planned out before we left Britain to set off on our European travels that reliable, dependable old Bill would get himself to Oulton Park fantastically early on the Monday morning to reserve us a nice spot in the paddock. Having driven overnight from Germany, we would then get set up in time for Clive to take part in the morning practice session (at 8am!). He would then have some much-needed sleep, before getting up to win the race in the afternoon. And that was pretty close to what happened, only with a little added team Horton drama en route.

Clive drove our huge Fiat van across Europe to Calais and onto the ferry, and then he drove us off the boat in Dover while I wrangled the children and got them into bed and all tucked in. Then I took over driving the beast while Clive tried to grab some shut-eye, leaving instructions that we would need diesel before reaching London, but not to turn the engine off because the starter motor was on its way out. An hour or so later I pulled into a petrol station and forgetfully turned the engine off. Drat! Or words to that effect. Clive filled the tank, paid, and hopped back in, and with a prayer I turned the ignition key. No go. The van wouldn't start. Double drat! (actually much worse things were said).

The character of Obergruppenfurher Horton then emerged. He does well to hide his schizophrenia but sometimes it's impossible, and he very calmly told me the only solution was to bump start our monster-sized, 3.5 ton, four-litre schweinhund of a truck. I was instructed to put it into second gear with the ignition switched on, and to dump the clutch only when instructed. Then I was to depress the pedal again only when the engine fired. 'Do NOT cock it up,' he added. 'This is our only chance.'

We only had ten yards for Clive to push the van up to speed, after that it was all uphill, so if it didn't start first time we were in deep trouble. He puts me under immense pressure sometimes and I usually come up with the goods. This was such an example. Hooray! It all went swimmingly, and he was so proud of me too. I could see it in his demeanour as he hopped back in the cab. That and the fact he kept muttering 'What a gall,' as he nodded off to sleep. Most gratifying.

I wasn't confident I knew the route, to be honest, although I understood we had to head roughly north, and that the M6 featured for a while, so I just got on with it the best I could and it was a mighty relief when we sailed past Fort Dunlop and I knew we were right on track. Soon after this psychological boost the sun came up and we were in Cheshire, and while Clive snoozed on I latched onto an ambulance, reasoning, perhaps a little blackly, that it was probably going to Oulton Park for the day. Suddenly our rider woke up, shouting, 'Where are we? I don't recognise this, we are lost! This isn't right, Bill won't be in the paddock,' and similar further torrents of negativity. I calmly replied, 'Actually, we are just turning into the circuit.' That sat him up I'll tell you.

And of course, Bill was there waiting, right on the money. What a guy. I knew he would be, he is so completely solid. Clive reckons he is such a good bloke you could call him on the phone and say: 'Bill, I'm desperate and I need your help. Meet me under the town hall clock in Aberdeen at noon tomorrow,' then slam the phone down. He would be there on time and simply say, 'What's all this about then?'

Everything went according to plan. Clive won the race, breaking Mike Hailwood's long-standing 250cc lap record in the process. Mike's circuit record, set on his Honda 6 in the mid 60s, was always considered a bit dodgy because it had stood for so long. We all assumed it had been down to a timekeeper with an itchy trigger finger. Of course, on the other hand, SMB Hailwood was something of a genius!

Clive said that on one lap he turned round to look behind (a very rare occurrence), and all he saw was a pair of very focused and determined beady eyes staring darkly at him across the top of Charlie Williams' fuel tank. 'Crikey!' he thought, 'Charlie looks like he means it today!' Ah but Clive meant it too. He got his head down and left Charlie well behind. Another 'nothing left in the tin' day.

Charlie Williams was a good guy and Clive and I liked and respected him a great deal. Clive and Charlie battled against each other a lot and although they never gave each other a millimetre, I was always comfortable watching them. They were never going to bring each other down. Clive was also incredibly impressed by Charlie chasing Mike Hailwood and Alex George hard all the way in the 1979 Classic TT. It was a great race, a classic in fact. But people forget Mike was on an RG500 Suzuki and Alex was on a 1000cc Honda, while Charlie was only on a 350. He didn't beat them, but he was right up their pipe. Fantastic. Charlie was a good diplomat too, unlike Clive on occasion! That's part of the reason why he got works rides for Honda. He fitted in as well as having talent. When Clive went to London to get his prize for winning the Honda 125 championship, Charlie and Stan Woods were also down there because of their successes on Honda endurance bikes. Phil Read was there too because people always invited Phil to things and he's usually up for a free night out.

Anyway, Gerald Davison the big boss of Honda invited the others out for dinner at the rooftop restaurant at the Hilton hotel, but not Clive. But Charlie insisted Clive went along and he sorted it all out, no bother. Clive had a great evening and had a really good chat with Phil Read, who was one of his idols. Good old Charlie!

But while Charlie was as safe as houses on the track, there were a few wild ones out there, riders that once Clive had passed them he'd look back at and think, 'Cripes, I'm off, I don't want him anywhere near me. I don't want to die thanks to that twit.' We got to know who the idiots were. Their balls were bigger than their brains, which was always a dangerous combination on the racetrack. Coming across them in a race would spur Clive on.

You needed to match your bravery with your ability. Sometimes you'd borrow a bit of extra bravery, but you'd have to pay it back later! But there were one or two on the British scene who had a permanent imbalance and thought it was all about being brave. Of course, when you get to the last lap all racers turn into pirates. They put their blades in their mouths and they are the boarding party. Nothing is ever given away on the last lap.

At Grand Prix level Clive reckoned everybody was good to be with and he knew they'd all do the right thing. Nobody would do anything desperate or stupid. He said it was a beautiful feeling, sharing the same small place on the planet, but giving each other space at the same time. Such trust and understanding was confidence-inspiring. I remember Clive coming in after coming across Clive Padgett on the track and racing against him properly for the first time. He said he was dead comfortable with him. That came from mutual respect. For reasons of reputation, there were some riders people were a little timid around. Clive was never in that category as far as I was aware but he tells me now that as his career went on it occurred to him being seen as uncompromising was not necessarily a bad thing, so tried to curry a reputation for being a bit hard on the track. Sometimes he tells me stuff now and I think good grief, it's a good job I didn't know about that at the time!

Dave, the boss, Orton suggested that Noddy should let Clive have a try-out on his 'spare' Suzuki RG500. 'See how you go,' said Dave. Well, Clive absolutely loved it, and his times were good enough for Dave to suggest he had a race or two on it. We used it only twice, winning first time out in the first ever 750cc race at the re-opened Donington Park. The regular big bike riders did nothing to gain Clive's respect as he found himself passing them in droves while still learning the bike. What baffled him most of all was that when he passed them all, making his way to the front, almost without exception they 'stayed passed'.

He couldn't get his head around this. If you pass someone in a lightweight race they take it as an affront and immediately bite back, re-passing or at least trying to. Not the big bike riders, it seems. They appeared to be completely preoccupied with riding their bikes and were too fully engaged in this to get into a scrap. Ron Haslam was the only one to put up a fight but he out-braked himself entering the Park Chicane and that was the last he saw of him. Clive won embarrassingly easily.

Clive on his way to a debut win on John Newbold's 'spare' Applby Glade Suzuki RG500

Clive's next 500cc outing was in an international event, again at Donington. The calibre of rider was far higher here, and we were all rather impressed with his progress during practice. He qualified near the front of the grid with established stars on either side and Barry Sheene directly in front of him! I can't remember the result, to be honest, but again, he did better than he or anyone else expected. He never did alter his view about heavy bike riders. He thinks the capacity of a rider's bike is usually inversely proportional to the size of his penis!

At the last event of the season, held once again at Brands Hatch, the 1980 Vladivar Vodka 250cc British Championship was on a knife edge. Going into the last round, Clive and Steve Tonkin were the only two riders with any chance of winning it. To come out on top Clive had to win the race gaining maximum points, and Tonks had to finish third or worse. Any other result and Tonks would be crowned champion.

Steve Tonkin from up in Cumbria, is a nice regular bloke and he was a really good rider, particularly on road circuits. Clive had a number of close races with him over the years. He stayed at his house once and was amazed when his girlfriend blew his porridge cool for him. Now that was a bit odd!

Clive qualified on the front of the grid but made his usual poor start. The conditions were not great, it must be said, a bit damp and slithery, and most sensible riders were out on intermediate tyres. As the race settled down he could see Steve ahead, obviously struggling with nerves and going quite slowly. 'I could see him up front and he looked so ruddy uncomfortable,' said Clive. I thought the poor sod, and I felt really sorry for him. I just got stuck in.'

Clive gained confidence from that and pressed on, catching and passing everyone including Steve and taking the lead. Clive said: 'Two corners from the chequered flag I glanced behind and saw Steve stuck behind another rider, and I thought, Oh smashing, the gods of racing still love me.' But when Bill greeted him after the slow-down lap, he grabbed the bike, breaking the bad news that Steve had managed to pass the guy between them and had achieved the second place he needed to take the title.

Ah, so the racing gods had only been flirting with us. The news failed to wipe the smile from Clive's face, however, as it was yet another of those 'nothing left in the tin' moments. You go out and do everything you can possibly do, but sometimes it still ain't enough!

Once the season was over Dave Orton dissolved his Appleby Glade racing set-up, which was a body blow for us all. He had enjoyed his most successful season as a sponsor, and he liked his riders as much as they liked him. The sidecar nutters even became British Champions! So why did he walk away from success like that? Because he was fed up to the back teeth with petty officialdom, and with organisers and circuit owners being constantly on the make. He was forever having to pay extra for this and fork out more for that. The powers that be at one circuit wanted him to pay £200 to fly his Appleby Glade flag on the flag pole attached to his own caravan!

All Dave ever wanted was a reasonable allocation of tickets so he could take his business associates to the races, something he enjoyed greatly. What the circuit owners and others failed to see was that by funding his teams to such a good standard Dave Orton was investing his money in THEIR businesses more than in his own. His expenditure for the season was something between fifty and a hundred thousand pounds, but still they wanted more. All he wanted was a few tickets. Not beautiful damsels scattering rose petals in front of him as he walked through the paddock! Not much to ask, and through greed and petty mindedness the sport lost a great man and a true benefactor.

Randy Racing

W e never starved during the off seasons, but it was sometimes a close run thing! We did a little motor trading, selling the odd 'banger' for Robin, and a bit of Del Boy-style ducking and diving too. One of our regular winter activities was taking a small stand at the annual Racing Motorcycle Show to sell brake pads for EBC. It was generally great fun, and we sold loads of them and made a few quid at the same time.

The winter of 1980/81 saw us getting stuck in to all our usual enterprises, and additionally Clive did some car repairs for a chap called John Chapman, but known to us as 'Superfan'. John was a local car dealer and we became friends through his love of racing. He knew how tough life could be for a racer and to help us out he offered Clive some employment. John 'Superfan' Chapman and his family, never missed a race meeting in England. He always took his caravan to the track for the duration, and the whole family were massive fans and steeped in the sport. They understood the ins and outs of racing and knew all the history, and they could recognise every rider from a glimpse of his helmet. A super family of real superfans.

One of the more memorable cars we sold was a Sunbeam Rapier, a model that was expensive to run and insure so we didn't expect a quick sale, and the fact this one had a ruddy great painting of an Eagle on its bonnet made us think we'd be stuck with it for months. Who the hell would buy something like that? We could not have been more wrong. We sold it almost immediately and the people who bought it absolutely loved it. Amazing! A car that was very hard for us to sell was surely a candidate for the worst car ever made: a pea-green air-cooled, twin cylinder thing that looked like an invalid carriage. It was a rubber band-drive DAF Variomatic.

Pea-green is not a popular colour. I read a children's book recently about a crayon called Pea-Green who complained bitterly about his name being disliked by everyone, and he insisted on being called 'Esteban the Magnificent'. Well, I don't think it would have been any easier to sell a DAF Variomatic if it was called Esteban the Magnificent, or if it had an eagle on its bonnet for that matter. The seating was a couple of deck chairs, and the heating and de-misting relied on the air that passed through the engine cooling ducts and was hit and miss to say the least. Wearing a big coat and keeping a sponge handy were the only effective ways of staying warm and seeing out of the windows. I sold it eventually, but what a load of rubbish! One of Clive's favourites was a Lancia Fulvia, a worn out Italian two-seater that was well past its best, but it must have been an absolute stunner in its day. What happened to it is lost in the mists of time. Coincidentally it was also in Esteban the Magnificent green!

The 1980 season had been a successful one, but once the racing was over Clive found himself unemployed once more, and with no prospects on the horizon. Pretty much the same situation as 12 months previously in many ways, but mentally he was in a very different place. All those positive 'selfs' were back! Only this time on turbo and in spades. The change in a rider's state of mind can be remarkable and instant after a race win or two, but depression can descend equally quickly.

I can't help but wonder where this 'stuff' comes from in the heads of sports people. They are all the same, I am certain: one day full of fragile self belief, and on another in need of a reassuring mental massage. As for which wins out more often, is it genetic? Is it good parenting? Bad parenting? Or purely the luck of the draw? I find it hard to say, but sportsmen and women are definitely wired up differently. There's something about their brain structure, I am certain of that. And it is not exclusive to sports people either.

Columbus, Rhodes, Nelson, WW2 Battle of Britain pilots and thousands of other intrepid types over the centuries have been driven by this 'stuff'.

At this time Clive was working some few days for Spondon Engineering, assisting in the development of their 250cc machine in the keen hope he would be riding it the following season. To achieve this, sponsorship would have to be be found. Bill Smith Motors was a sensible possibility, but Bill was very reticent about commitment, and vague reassurances were all that was forthcoming from the Chester Honda dealer.

Clive really liked Spondon Engineering's two directors, Bob 'Stevo' Stevenson and Stuart 'Stu' Tiller. He enjoyed being in the macho environment of the working man once again, complete with plenty of foul language flying around. Goodness me, or should I say ****
me, Bob could swear. In fact, he swore so much that to distinguish him from other, 'nicer' Bobs on the racing scene he was often called Sweary Bob. Nevertheless, he was universally loved and highly respected, a fact borne out by the large number of people that turned up for his funeral relatively recently.

The Racing Motorcycle Show was held at the old Birmingham Exhibition Centre in January 1981, the more usual Alexander Palace venue having been consumed by fire. We set up our little EBC brake pad stand and made a few quid as usual, but much bigger deals were in the wind. For a start, it was at this Birmingham show that the new Armstrong 250cc racer was first seen. That it was a beautiful and business-like machine is the first thing that must be said. It was the brainchild of an engineer from the by now demised Cotton concern, and it was built at the CCM factory in Bolton, Lancashire. At that time CCM was in the process of being taken over by Armstrong Engineering, who were shock absorber manufacturers. Everything was in a state of flux.

While we were on our stand serving customers, we were approached by a potential backer, a lovely man who wanted to give us £1,000 cash if we would spend time with him in his company's box at Donington during race meetings, chatting to his customers. How encouraging was that!

Then, soon afterwards, we were visited by a blonde, 40-ish female with huge self-confidence who introduced herself as Mrs Ruth Randle. I didn't like her it must be said, but Clive found her a formidable woman and I could see he was feeling confident again as the season drew nearer. He was absolutely full of it, in fact, but she stunned him by saying: 'I am the sponsor who will be backing the factory Armstrong team next year. What bikes do you need for next season?' 'W w w well...' he stammered. 'A 250 and a 350.' 'Very good,' she countered. 'Who will you be riding for?' 'It's not fully sorted out yet,' he bluffed, 'Probably Spondon engineering with support from Bill Smith.' 'Come and see me in hospitality on the Armstrong stand when you have a moment,' she said, and with that she turned on her high heels and was gone.

Our next visitor was Alan Clews the man behind CCM (Clews Competition Motorcycles), accompanied by the designer of the 250 Armstrong, Mike Eatough. They also asked Clive about his plans and what bikes he would be riding the next season. A little more composed this time, he replied: 'It doesn't really matter what bike I ride, I will be winning on it whatever it is!' I could see Alan was a little taken aback. I don't think he was expecting such a confident, almost swaggering, reply. But it must have left quite an impression as Clive subsequently received an invitation to Sunday lunch at Alan's home, together with two other potential members of the Armstrong team for 1981: Jeff Sayle, a world-class Australian rider, and Steve Tonkin, Clive's principal adversary the previous season.

Nothing was signed, sealed and delivered though, and we continued to look for support for the Spondon Engineering project. But then we were told Ruth Randle had been offered £10,000 by Armstrong if Clive would sign with them, joining Jeff and Steve, and that each rider would receive £2,000 as a signing on fee, leaving £4,000 towards the team's general expenses. Well, it had to be done which meant Clive had to walk out on his buddies at Spondon. And when he did the deed the silly bugger was moved to tears. Can you believe it? Mr swaggering, cock-strutting, super-sure of himself was actually crying because he felt he'd let his mates down. For those of us who had spent years eating grass clippings for sustenance, a £2,000 inducement looked mighty appealing, but quite honestly, compared with the money some riders were receiving, it was chicken feed. We know this because a few years later we had sight of a contract signed by a well-known star of the 1960s and 70s, and his sign-on fee was much more than ten times that of all three Armstrong boys put together. Compared with this, our package was indeed chicken feed. Never mind, Clive was so desperate for a competitive ride he would have signed for a jam sandwich. Yours truly, on the other hand, was nowhere near as keen. I did not entirely trust Ruth Randle. Yes, I had seen the movie 'The Good, the Bad and the Ugly', but I did not have full faith this particular 'Blondie' could be trusted to turn and shoot through the rope!

We had a team launch at the Randle homestead - the White House in Whitwick. It was a grand place with a swimming pool and some really big rooms. Several, let's call them 'celebrities', turned up and some of our friends too. Our old sponsor Robin came, and also our new personal sponsor from Wetterns builders' merchants in Nottingham. Phil Read, one of Ruth's 'boyfriends' (actually, there were not many blokes that weren't), promptly tried to chat this guy up for funds for his helicopter project, or whatever get rich quick scheme he was planning at the time. Ready was a six-time world champion in the 1960s and early 1970s and a class act, but always a bit of a baddie. Despite this, Clive had been a fan of Phil's for years.

Wally Wettern gave him the brush-off, anyway. His name wasn't Wally by the way. Wally was the company mascot - a logo in the form of a sea lion. I wish I could recall the chap's name; he was a really nice man, and I liked his wife too. When the season got going they would ask me to do my lap-scoring from their hospitality suite and although I much preferred to be in the pit lane or alone on a corner somewhere, they were really nice people and I sometimes felt obliged to take up their offer so they could feel more involved. Unfortunately, I hated it because it was really hard to concentrate with everyone asking me questions all the time and sticking drinks in front of me.

I enjoyed being with the other girls on the pit lane and we supported each other to a degree, but I used to prefer to go off on my own to do my timekeeping bit, away from all the distractions of the pits. Clive used to put me on corners and say, tell me what I'm doing wrong, or tell me what so and so's doing there, whatever he'd got a bee in his bonnet about that day. At Brands Hatch he'd often put me on Paddock Bend. I used to absolutely hate being there because it used to scare me so much. I still don't like watching them pile through there on the first lap when I watch BSB on the telly. I watch from between my fingers!

Oulton Park was always one of my favourite tracks. I could do my job quite easily there, because there were plenty of places I could watch from, and we always seemed to have a good weekend whenever we went there. There's a lot to it and it's in a lovely setting. It was a great track altogether, but perhaps less so now. If you put chicanes into a race track, you inevitably spoil it. I liked Cadwell Park too. I'd watch them come over the Mountain and then they'd disappear into Hall Bends and it took ages for them to reappear on the start-finish straight. It was the same every lap. 'Oh no, something's happened. Where the hell is he?' Or I'd watch from the start line, and as well as being able to get my times absolutely spot on I could get a fix on him at several different places around the track. I could see him come over the Mountain and know if both wheels were in the air he was really going for it.

At the Randle Armstrong team's launch party a TV company turned up and interviewed the manager and her riders. I stood in the background and, I don't mind admitting, slowly simmered. Ruth came across OK, brassy blondes rarely go far wrong in front of a camera, but then it was Jeff's turn and he was rather reticent and nervous, and his Aussie drawl was almost unintelligible. Next came Tonks, but he had a bit of a stammer at the best of times. I could see the whole thing going down the pan, and ending upon the editor's spike, or I should probably say the cutting room floor. But then they focused on Clive, who had been thinking exactly the same as me. So he hammed it up big time trying to rescue the situation, talking about riding on the Daytona banking and being horizontal to the earth! You could see the TV people's faces brighten immediately as they too had been losing the will to live.

In fact, they were so encouraged they had Clive act out a little scene in which the team departed in the van for the first event of the season. It made the news anyway, so it turned out ok, but it was quite amazing how much effort was expended for what ended up being just a few minutes' screen time.

We had a bit of previous experience with a TV crew. In the 1978 season Gary Newbon, who did a fair bit of front of camera sports presenting for ITV in those days, invited us to Donington Park with the Brader Brothers-sponsored bike to make a feature which showed us, and it, off to the wider British public. We were not allowed to use the full circuit that day, but we were permitted to make use of the historic Melbourne Loop section. Gary was also scheduled to do an interview with Pentti Airikkala, a top rally driver, but Pentti was running late. So Gary suggested we went to lunch and used the time to fill himself in with some useful background information before filming in the afternoon. We went to the Crewe and Harpur pub at Swarkestone Bridge by the River Trent.

Just as an aside, with due respect to history and all that, this Swarkestone Bridge marks the furthest point south that Bonnie Prince Charlie's Jacobite rebel forces ever reached in England. Teary-eyed Scots wax lyrically about Charlie, singing about his bonnie boat speeding over the sea to Skye as he scarpered from the English, but the boozer near Donington Park where we had our lunch that day is actually an equally important place in the young pretender's story. Apparently sometime in 1745 Charlie was ensconced in an Inn in Derby, just up the road, busy prattling away in Italian or French no doubt to anyone who'd listen (he didn't speak English, or, rather, Celtic). Meanwhile his scouts reached the river Trent at the very spot where the Crewe and Harpur now stands, only to detect a lack of support from the locals and hear tales of massed armies marching their way northwards.

The scouts duly lost their nerve and scuttled back to Derby, whereupon they regaled their leader with completely fanciful and fictitious tales of massed forces marching northwards against them. Whether there was anything to be immediately frightened of or not, their report spooked Charlie's generals enough to send the Jacobites jogging back up to sweaty sock-land. Charlie was eventually defeated at the Battle of Culloden the following April. So Swarkestone Bridge may be just a place on the map, but it has more significance than you'd think. And nearly 250 years later a statue of Bonny Prince on horseback was erected on Derby's Cathedral Green. Anyway, we got on well with Gary. He was very professional,

I thought, and he seemed keen to make his work as good as it possibly could be. I was clearly heavily pregnant at the time (with our daughter Emma), and Gary commented that his wife was expecting twins. It was nice to have some rapport. He enjoyed our company too, and a few days later we received a letter from him thanking us for an enjoyable and productive day. If I remember correctly, Pentti was a rather dull chap, a bit Finnish actually, so our piece brightened up what would have been a rather lacklustre item. Unfortunately we missed seeing our little film on the telly when it was aired as we were too busy roasting in the Marseilles sunshine.

Things became difficult between me and Clive when it was decided the Randle Armstrong team's first event would be the Daytona 200 meeting in Florida at the beginning of March. Riders only with no wives was the edict. But of course Ruth would be going and I wasn't at all happy about that. It wasn't right. It was indefensible, and I didn't trust her an inch.

She had already tried to organise a pre-season test session at Paul Ricard in the south of France with no wags in attendance, just her, the mechanics and riders. (I am chuffed to bits, by the way, for having this opportunity to use this term to describe myself!). I received anxious phone calls from Jeff's wife and Steve's girlfriend and I told them I was jolly well going whether she liked it or not. I was not being dictated to like that by a team manager. We three agreed to travel there together under our own steam, and when Ruth got wind of our plan the test session was abandoned.

Clive wasn't part of the team's Daytona line up at first as only the two blue-eyed boys were entered, but then Andy Freeman of EBC, that lovely man, volunteered to sponsor Clive for the trip, and his cash made his inclusion possible. Bill Bristow, our mechanic, paid for his own air tickets! Not exactly living the dream, but it was what it was, and we just had to get on with it.

Daytona

I didn't go to Daytona so I can't say anything further about it. I was as mad as hell, though! Apoplectic actually, and it set the tone and my low level of respect for the Randle Racing enterprise for the rest of the season. Clive takes over the story for a while from here as I know nothing first hand about the goings-on on this American adventure, and I carry feelings of resentment and loathing about it to this day.

Clive: *We flew with Pan Am to Miami (several years before Lockerbie of course). Ruth rented a car, and our team of three riders and female manager all travelled together, staying the first night at a Ramada Inn. It was here that I realised Sue's suspicions about Ruth were justified, as she spent the night in the same room as one of the other two riders. I won't use the term 'slept together' as this euphemism for shagging misses the mark by a million miles. I was a bit shocked if I'm honest. We all do a bit of flirting and mucking about, but actually shagging? Well, it's more than just deceitful. There were four people involved, don't forget: the two protagonists, of course, and also their partners - unwitting victims left at home. However, you just have to shrug your shoulders and get on with life. It is what it is.*

The mechanics rented a U-haul and travelled with our designated guide, a journalist called Martin Christie. He was useless as a guide, but a nice bloke. I liked him. They picked up the bikes from the airport and drove them the 200 miles to Daytona. American trucks are a bit rough and ready, lacking the sophistication of the European ones, but you can pull trees down with them if things get desperate. So they crunched the gears and ground their way northwards. We had a lovely ride in comparison and we all met up at the Howard Johnson Motel on Speedway Boulevard, where Bill and I shared a room (not for the first time you will recall).

I absolutely loved Daytona. To race there had always been an ambition of mine, a dream, even. In the 1970s and 1980s all the big hitters did this prestigious season opener in the Florida sunshine. The high speeds on the banking were such a thrill, and racing in the sun under clear blue skies was always a treat, although the locals said it was cold. Not to us. Since when has 80 degrees Fahrenheit been cold to a Brit? It was like coming out of a coma for most of us.

We were allocated a garage and the bikes were unloaded and assembled. We looked absolutely the dog's danglers as a team. The bikes were freshly-painted in smart yellow and blue livery, we had three eager riders all dressed to kill, and a blonde team manager in heels! We were the talk of the town. Our main competitor would seem to be a certain Eddie Lawson (soon to become 500cc world champion, a feat he would then repeat three more times). Lawson was riding a works 250cc Kawasaki, and I actually passed him down the back straight in practice. That made me smile, I don't mind telling you. But then we ran into a major technical difficulty.

We had taken a supply of our favourite slick tyres made by Dunlop. These were not generally available at this race track, i.e. there was no Dunlop tyre service for our class, and we were not amused to be informed by the officials that we could not continue to use our own Dunlops. The reason? 'All tyres have to be freely available to all competitors. Read the regulations: page 621, subsection two, paragraph four, line four!' Well, something like that. You know what I mean. The upshot was we had to use Goodyears like everyone else. Damn it.

The Goodyears were of a different profile, which made our bikes ride lower to the ground. We had, in fact, on first seeing the machines at the CCM factory, remarked on how low to the ground the exhaust tailpipe and silencer were on the right side. The designer had said 'Worry n̶   have done tests with the suspension lowered to its maximum and the pipe doesn't ground until you are so far over you will have crashed anyway.' Already, I am sure some of you are thinking, 'Famous last words.' Your instinct is correct.

Eddie came over to reassure us about the Goodyears. He said he had been using them for ages and they were perfectly fine and that we had no need to be concerned. It may be hard to imagine a fellow competitor doing this, especially one as competitive as Eddie, but it is quite common behaviour in motorcycle racing even at this high level. Indeed, it is this sort of special extra something that makes the lunacy of bike racing so enjoyable.

Out on the track practice continued and although we struggled to start with, we soon got to grips with the Goodyears' characteristics, and I was helped in this by Eddie when he came past me braking hard for a corner on the infield, riding with aplomb and displaying his absolute faith in the tyres. Yes, the tyres were fine actually, but my tailpipe came back with a few light scuffs on it so I was still slightly concerned. Oh well, I thought, the racing gods will deal with it.

There were qualifying heats and a final in those days, and we all qualified well enough. I can't recall our grid placings but Jeff, due to some technical issue or other, was reduced to the second wave, the grid being split into two groups, started ten seconds apart. No worries though, as the 250cc race was a 100 miler in those days. Off we went, and after about three laps I was getting a little frustrated with my progress, or lack of it. This sometimes happens in a race, and you have to shake yourself out of your malaise and get properly stuck in. So I did, and entering the chicane (a cheap circuit modification created using straw bales and designed to slow everybody down on the back straight for safety reasons) I decided to come out fighting. Sadly, I didn't come out of the chicane at all. I grabbed a big handful of throttle while cranked over and the tailpipe touched down big time,

prominent hooter, it is a physical requirement, I find. Anyway, I kept whacking 30-grade sunscreen on it, and by the end of the day I had a white nose and a red face and looked a complete twerp.

One of the reasons I lost a bit of interest in the team was the fact that after Daytona Jeff was going straight off with his bike to the first grand prix of the year in Argentina. Not me though, I was off home. Poor management, I thought, and it created a bad team vibe. I didn't blame Jeff. Why would I? But he was the team's bluest of blue-eyed boys, and I needed his scalp!

A final footnote from me: when Jeff got back to the UK, he told us he had seen the first production Armstrongs, and that they had modified tailpipe silencers. That drew an ironic smile.

Of course, while all the above was taking place, I received only my statutory single telephone call. Just the one, and from a gas station call box near the HoJo. Just ten dollars-worth and all of a rush, true to form. For my part, I had been in contact with Dave 'Big Daddy' Orton who had a twin-engined four-seater company aeroplane with a pilot. He arranged for me to fly in and meet the team at Gatwick and fly back with them to East Midlands Airport. I took Ruth's husband along with me who then drove them home in a Cadillac. Crikey! Did I mention I had become a jet setter? It did cost a fair few quid though, as the landing fees at Gatwick alone made your eyes water. As it turned out we had to queue in the sky above Gatwick waiting for their plane from Florida to land before we could. Life is all about timing, it seems.

The Randle years

Sharing the winner's car during a lap of honour. Clip-board still in hand. I look rather chuffed

The Randle Armstrong team performed well in the UK, but never quite reached its potential in the Grands Prix. At the French Grand Prix at Paul Ricard (subsequently one of Clive's favourite circuits), he failed to qualify, not helped by having a massive practice crash at the fast chicane that follows the start and finish line. Clive was having difficulty there and he didn't know why, so he asked the bike's designer (who had flown out to the event with the Armstrong MD) to observe at that section and see if he had any ideas.

It was an important corner taken in fifth gear at well over a hundred miles an hour. In Clive went, but out he did not come. Just trying too hard out of frustration I guess. It was a whopper of a crash and he slid for ages down the track and into the gravel. And when he eventually stopped and staggered to his feet he found he was dressed only in his boots, underpants and back protector. His leather suit was shredded and hanging around his ankles. Clive was carted off to the medical centre but there was little in the way of physical injuries. Nonetheless he was shocked, shaken and generally battered. The bike needed surgery, and he needed some time to recover.

The destroyed leather suit warrants further mention. It was made from goat skin and had been supplied by the same Welsh company that made his Appleby Glade leathers the previous year, Cambrian Fashions. The Appleby Glade suits were the first motorcycle racing outfits the firm had ever made, and they had used American steer hide. Talk about tough! They were fantastic! For this year, though, they had stuck their necks out and gone for goat skin. Apparently it has special properties and was often used for running shoes because it is highly resistant to piercing by running spikes. It is also soft and pliable. Clive will believe anything, especially if you can nail a piece of dodgy science to it, and it was lovely tactile stuff too. But after the shredding incident at Paul Ricard, we thought American steer hide had the edge over goat skin in terms of rider safety to be honest.

Bill and Clive rebuilt the bike but it didn't help and he didn't qualify. Jeff qualified OK, so perhaps he was a bit smarter on the set-up front. What was needed, Clive now reckons, was a lifting up of the rear and a lowering of the front, to give less castor enabling a quicker turn. But we didn't have that level of technical understanding back then. Nor did the bike's designer, it appears. He offered no solution and despite being detailed to observe Clive he never even saw the crash. He said he was busy watching the young German star Martin Wimmer at the time! Now, you say, just one job, you only had one job! So why oh why didn't you do it? We exit stage left with a gallic shrug.

The team did look good from the outside though, and all three riders won races and had some good battles over the years. One such was a dead-heat between Clive and Tonks, brought about mainly due to Clive having made his usual poor start and then having to hack his way through the field. Tonks was leading and Clive caught him on the final lap, at which point Steve turned round and waved him to stay back! Clive was not amused. 'Stay back? After I have ridden like a demon, chopped and sliced my way to the front? You must be joking.' He drew alongside Tonks at the final corner and they drag-raced to the line. Clive won he is sure. Tonks thought he had too, of course, but Ruth was in the timekeepers' office and suggested it may well have been a dead heat. Politically expedient perhaps, but I was as mad as hell. Clive had clearly won. The cow! My reaction to this incident did nothing to help endear me to Ruth and the rest of the team.

Then there was the time we entered an international street race meeting in Holland. Only Bill and Clive went, and I stayed at home. Nothing spectacular seemed to be on the cards. The bike ran OK during practice, and Clive qualified in the middle of the grid. A dead average performance from both bike and rider. Overnight Clive and Bill stripped and rebuilt the engine as was routine, finding nothing wrong or untoward. All in all, rather boring.

But in the race Clive and the Armstrong both performed extraordinarily! Clive was passing people for fun down the straights and with the bike so on song and inspiring him all the more, he out-braked, out-cornered and generally out-rode the opposition. He won spectacularly, and Bill said: 'He came through the pack like a dose of salts, I was signalling and I could hardly keep up. I was chucking numbers about all over the place and it was a great ride. I loved it.'

Shortly after the race finished I received a telephone call from Holland. No, not a quick update from him, it was from Roel, the guy who had taken Daniel to lost property a few years before. Since that day, he had become our special Dutch friend, and his first words down the phone were: 'You'll get flowers.' That's all I could make out and I was thrown into a bit of a panic, quite frankly. I thought Clive had been killed and he was phoning to tell me to get ready for a funeral.

Wonderful tool that it is, the brain works through information like lightning and makes connections. Unfortunately, or fortunately in this case, they are sometimes the wrong connections. After a few more words and a mental re-sort, I realised Roel was telling me Clive had won some flowers, that he would be bringing flowers home for me. Dear oh dear. The wringer you put yourself through as the 'girl back home'. Wives and girlfriends are better off at the trackside any day.

Roel also told me Clive had successfully collected his start and prize money. Unlike most riders at the meeting, Clive had to leave the track early to get home for another race the following day. This meant he had to collect his cash from the organisers before the meeting ended, and before anyone else, and then he and Bill would have to cross fields and dykes to escape from the circuit and get out onto the roads and away.

The plan worked and the boys were on the ferry home before the race organisers found they had not taken enough gate money to pay all the riders in full. That is the problem with meetings on public roads where the organisers are trying to charge entrance money but people can just turn up and sneak in o'er field and glen. We had lost out in these circumstances before, and we were fortunate not to be on the losing side this time.

Despite my antipathy we did another season with the Randle set-up, there being nothing much else on the table. The bikes improved slightly on the handling front following a change to the steering head angle, and a newly-developed 350cc Armstrong machine was added to the stable, specifically for Clive to ride. It was another in-line twin, and altogether largely similar to the 250, but slightly more agricultural, Clive found.

But it did pack a punch, and it was fitted with an Armstrong shock absorber built by some boffins who had worked with Jackie Stewart in F1. The bike's chief designer had insisted that as road racing took place on relatively smooth surfaces, unlike motocross, there needn't be much pressure in the shocker. Clive found the 350 gave a very smooth but generally uninformative and unfeeling ride. Eventually, after trying this and that, the ex-F1 boffins said, 'why not follow our hunch and try more pressure. Let's just give it a go?' They did and Clive went out at Donington Park and broke the lap record. What an easy fix! Let's leave it to the technical boffins and not the theorists in future.

Unfortunately, the 350cc engine had a design fault and regularly broke crank pins. Whenever Clive rode the bigger bike he was either first or second, or he broke down, but he loved the bike. Even after it seized its gearbox at the very fast, very hazardous NorthWest 200 street circuit.

A gearbox seizure on a racing motorcycle is one of the worst things that can ever happen. The rear wheel locks suddenly and completely, and an instantaneous lack of control usually brings about a huge crash. There is absolutely nothing the rider can do, and because speeds are generally very high when such catastrophic seizures occur, with the gearbox under massive stress, fatalities often result. Clive was always a jammy so and so. When he had the gearbox seizure at the NorthWest 200 he simply lost drive on the start and finish straight and slowed gracefully to a stop. The back wheel didn't actually lock up solid until he was pushing the bike back along the pavement!

He has not been so lucky with money, however. We have never had particularly good fortune in that area, generally losing it rather than accumulating it. Still, if you are due a set quota of luck, better to use it up on the race track, rather than in the stock market, I would say.

The 1982 NorthWest 200 was a particularly sad meeting for us. John Newbold, that lovely, sometimes daft, happy-go-lucky, funny guy we got to know during our Appleby Glade days, was killed dicing with Mick Grant. It depressed us hugely and left such a bitter taste we never returned to the event. So many riders have lost their lives there. So many tragedies. But on the upside, the Irish love a funeral.

Steve Henshaw was another good friend of ours. A lovely funny guy, and a solid individual. We loved him, really. He was at the NorthWest 200 with us when John Newbold was killed and his wife, Val, pleaded with him not to go out afterwards because we'd just lost

John. Steve did race, but he said: 'If me not racing today would bring John back, I would never race again for the rest of my life.' We thought that was a fabulous statement, so positive and typical of him. Racers are not the lunatics some people might think.

When Steve was killed at the TT seven years later Val was in the pit lane, and as had happened to me, the clocks stopped moving. But tragically an official eventually came over to see her, and said: 'I'm really sorry Val, but we've lost him this time.' Then she had to go to the hospital where she was met by two guys wearing leathers, carrying flowers, and they all put their heads together and cried.

Clive says losing friends is all part of life's training scheme. It's all a process that prepares you to die. When you're young, you think you'll never die, that you'll live forever, and then when you get to your fifties and early sixties, you think well yes, we are going to die, and then after it's been accepted you have come to terms with it. And part of the process is when googlies are thrown in like losing John Newbold and Steve Henshaw. Woof! It can happen anytime, and it sends you reeling a bit.

Our leaving the NorthWest for the final time signalled the start of another Horton transportation saga. We had to dash back home overnight to race at Donington Park the following day, and we were in a big rush to catch the ferry from Belfast for the four-hour crossing to Stranraer, Scotland. We didn't have time to stop for diesel on the Irish side of the North Sea, and we knew we were pushing it a bit, but we thought we would pick some up on the other side. No worries. Stranraer was a busy commercial port, with lorries going hither and yon; we would be OK, we felt. Ruth was travelling with us, as was Bill, and we had our two children aboard, so we were a bit full to say the least.

It was pitch black when we landed in Scotland at about 11pm, and deadly quiet with no gas stations open. There was bound to be one somewhere en route, we reasoned. No worries, let's just press on. We were wrong. Nothing was open anywhere and as the miles rolled by we started to feel very uneasy. The route from Stranraer must be the bleakest, darkest, most sinister, ghostly, tree-lined, God-forsaken route on planet earth.

We were desperate and the tension was mounting among the van's adult passengers. Not the children though, they were sleeping. But we were getting optimistic sounds from our driver. Clive was driving very economically, freewheeling down the hills, and using the smallest of throttle openings wherever possible. 'Something will be around the next corner,' he kept saying, and other such wishful remarks, but then the engine spluttered to silence and we coasted to a halt. Drat and double drat! We were on a deserted country road in the early hours of a Sunday morning with no civilisation in sight. We decided to snuggle down and sleep as there was nothing else we could do. We would have to miss the meeting at Donington and our chance to scoop some decent winnings there.

Clive hopped down from the cab and stood on the roadside, willing a fellow traveller to come to our rescue. He does have a bit of a knack when it comes to this sort of thing, I will admit. 'You can't always get what you want, but if you try, sometimes, well, you may find you get what you need,' (© Rolling Stones 1969), and this uncanny gift has never left him.

An aside: many years later we were walking the Pennine Way, lost in the fog on Kinder Scout without a clue where we were going, and this was only our first day! We were, for some unfathomable reason, following a stream in the hope of resetting our mental GPS. Furthermore, Clive was in a diabetic glucose deficit. I should have noticed sooner as he was becoming more stupid by the minute

179

(although it can be difficult to tell sometimes!) but I was too cheesed off to give the matter any thought. Then suddenly, out of the mist, striding manfully, came the figure of Jesus!

Our saviour was wearing hiking boots, not sandals, so he was a bit off-script, and he was striding along by himself without a disciple in sight. It must have been the son of God. Who else would wander about on Kinder Scout in thick fog, entirely on their own? Of course, he knew exactly the way we wanted to go and he led us back onto the right path, before heading off in another direction, muttering something about loaves and fishes or water and wine as the fog closed back around him. May blessings and peace be upon him!

He did not appear in this Scottish hellhole, however. No chance! Dawn was approaching when headlamps were glimpsed and a van slowly strained its way towards us and stopped. Incredibly, it contained a group of bike race fans carrying a spare can of diesel which they insisted we used, taking no money for it at all as they were pleased to be able to assist a racing team. And before we could set off on our way a lorry appeared and its helpful driver gave us a spare can of red diesel he was carrying for his refrigeration system. He too waived payment, being just happy to help. Thanks to these gifts we had enough fuel for 40 more miles, and before too long a gas station duly appeared where we could fill the tank. I said Clive was a jammy so-and-so!

When we arrived at Donington Park it was nearly lunchtime and practice was completely finished, but the organisers very kindly let Clive have a ride round the circuit in the lunch break. A practice session all to himself! Those of you who are familiar with race organisers can be forgiven for doubting this actually happened, but I can assure you it did. Sometimes there are advantages in being a local lad liked by the club secretary.

Sadly the story ends in anticlimax. All that effort - the dash to the ferry, the long drive, the breakdown, the salvation, the race to the circuit, the being greeted as local hero and long-lost son, the privileged practice session and special treatment allowing him to start - and the day ended in utter embarrassment. The dratted bike failed on the start line and would not run again. As the rest of the field completed their first lap, Clive dumped the silent Armstrong at the side of the track and trudged disconsolately back to the pits.

Another story I can recall involving help from a friendly race secretary was when a new edict was issued regarding pit lane safety. No children under 16 were to be allowed in the pit lane at Donington Park on Fuhrer's orders! Now my children had been in pit lanes since being born, and they knew exactly how to behave. At this time they were six and four-years-old and they could be trusted to sit still on a set of fixed chairs at the trackside. It was part of our routine. Lo and behold, along came a member of the track security staff who told Clive the kids would have to leave. He firmly told the fellow they would be staying put. That they would not be running about in the pit lane, and they were perfectly safe. The official then climbed up on his high horse and insisted they leave, right now.

'Have you got a gun?' Clive shouted. 'No, why?' 'Well you will need one to get me to shift them.' Things were getting heated and the enraged feldwebel stomped off to seek advice from the circuit top brass who presumably told him to leave it. Just ignore it, pretend you haven't noticed, or words to that effect.

By now Daniel had started school, and when we raced abroad I'd take him out for a week, or a fortnight, because you could in those days. All the teachers knew about Clive's racing and in their own way they did their bit to back us. They used to get very excited. 'How did you get on?' that sort of thing. I said to Daniel's teacher one day, do you think it's doing him any harm taking him off with us, and she said, 'He'll learn far more travelling around Europe with you than staying here.' And I'm sure she was right. All that travelling, all those countries, mixing with people of different nationalities, playing with foreign kids.

Later on in that year, at Snetterton, we had a bit of a nasty moment. As a gift for Daniel, Clive had purchased, or perhaps traded for a bag of crisps, a small, home-built motorcycle. I was not amused. It was a death trap and I said so.

At race meetings, in the evenings after practice was over, our Dan and Ruth's son Timmy would often go off exploring on their minibikes. One such evening I was cooking dinner while Clive was working on an engine in the back of the van when we noticed the blues and twos of an ambulance leaving the paddock. Most unusual at that time of day and I had an uneasy premonition. I felt a wave of concern. Then someone bashed on the side of the van and told us Daniel had crashed into the ambulance while riding his minibike and had been rushed to Norwich hospital. We had to abandon our tasks and chase after it to find out what had happened. What were his injuries? What would be the implications? It was a horrible half-hour ride.

Poor Daniel. His face was terribly smashed in and he looked an awful mess. But it could have been much worse. Thank goodness we always insisted he wore a helmet. What had happened, apparently, was the throttle had stuck open and he hadn't known what to do. He was only six. The bike had careered out of control with him on it and stuffed itself into the front wing of the ambulance. Fortunately, the wing was made of fibreglass, so it had absorbed the impact quite well. A pre-crumple-zone, crumple-zone! Daniel recovered after a few days, and we paid £125 for repairs to the ambulance. After that I put my foot down and we sold the death trap. But we kept the boy!

Sunset for a wannabe

Writing the previous chapter has brought another event back to mind, one that is quite poignant, as it happens.

We had been at Paul Ricard some years before when disturbing news reached us on the paddock grapevine (the news system in those days was word of mouth - no Facebook or Twitter back then, of course). A young boy riding his bike around the paddock in the dark had collided with a washing line, nearly garrotting himself and crashing in the process. His name - Alan Carter!

Thank goodness the lad survived the incident without permanent injury, and a few seasons later, still only 16 years of age, and not put off motorcycles one bit, he had become very fast on racing motorcycles. In fact, beating young Alan started to become quite a challenge for my 32-year-old 'veteran'. The lad always started brilliantly and scorched off like greased lightning, and Clive was finding it it impossible to make the deficit up. Alan was on an Armstrong, too, so the factory started asking questions, and loving the new guy more than our man.

Word reached us Armstrong had put Alan's engine on the factory dynamometer and its measured power output was 68bhp. Our so-called 'official' factory bike had never been assessed, so when the Armstrong management started demanding to know why we were getting beaten by a 16-year-old, Clive said: 'Well, put our bike on the dyno too, and let's see where we are.' Our bike only managed 58bhp. There you go, Alan was a flyweight in those days, but much more of a factor was that his bike was producing more than 20% more power! Clive relayed this to CCM boss Alan Clews who said: '10bhp That's sweet FA.' Now I knew nothing about football, but I didn't agree with his assessment!

Things went downhill from there until the end of the season. We had lost all enthusiasm for being in the team, and the team had lost interest in us. Ruth did manage to winkle the 250 out of the factory for Clive to keep as a severance payment, and I have to give her due credit for that. It would be crucial too, as it turned out, as we would be on our own again the following season. Ultimately, the factory Armstrong was a big let-down, as so many things in life are! But no regrets. We had little choice. It's not as if there were lots of other offers on the table.

Little Alan Carter went on to win a Grand Prix in 1983 and ride Yamahas for Kenny Roberts the following year. He has recently written his autobiography and a good read it is too!

I'm afraid any mention of Ruth Randle makes my hackles go up to this day. Her main interest was getting off with other people's husbands and she didn't seem to care what harm that caused, nor how it hurt her own husband, Richard. She was having HRT treatment and she never wasted an opportunity to tell everyone who'd listen how, because of this, she was permanently up for it. She had a long-term relationship with Jeff Sayle and multiple other affairs and one night stands at the same time.

Clive beat Jeff several times, but he thinks Jeff had a slight edge on him overall, reckoning he didn't have to work quite as hard to get his results. And although he didn't allow himself to like him too much while they were racing against each other, he now says Jeff was a really nice bloke. But how can that be if he was bedding Randle? His wife found out about the affair eventually, or perhaps she knew all along. Whatever, she surprised me and several other wives one day by calmly announcing they would soon be going back to Australia, because of 'all that has been happening between Ruth and Jeff'. Our jaws dropped.

Ruth was the Randle Racing figurehead, but it was her husband Richard's money that bankrolled the team. Richard sold furniture and TVs in the Leicestershire town of Coalville and he was a big hitter there. I think blondie thought she'd have some of that and latched onto him.

Later on when Richard left her high and dry it made my day. He wasn't stupid. He knew what was going on and he bided his time and organised his finances so that when the time was right he was able to leave her for someone else. The last time we saw Richard he was ill with Parkinson's, but as far as I know he had a happy relationship second time around. He is a good human being and a decent man, and I'm glad it worked out for him.

The demise of Randle Armstrong was pretty much the end of our Grand Prix adventures. It had been fun, it had become part of our lives, and we were part of the hierarchy. It's interesting, you're not a full member of the GP paddock until you're in your second year because you could be just blowing through. You're not truly accepted until sometime in the second season. We were always among the poor people, of course, not being part of a big works team or having a hugely wealthy backer. But despite that you got accepted by everyone once you'd done your time, and for a good number of years we'd been part of a special group.

Chas Mortimer had become a good friend over the years and we would end up going into business with him. By the end of the Randle era we had both been working for his Chas Mortimer Racing School for a couple of years. Clive was an instructor, and I typed up a report for each client at the end of each day's training. It was a successful business and jolly good fun. We worked at several different circuits, met lots of interesting people, and had a damn good time together.

One of Clive's pupils had an extra-special day at Goodwood when, following the teacher, he had a perfect view as Clive's bike seized solid and chucked him off. Clive was knocked unconscious and had to be taken to hospital in Chichester. We had to miss a race meeting the following day as a result but Ruth was quite sympathetic and understanding about it. It takes time to recover from concussion, not at all like it is in the movies when the hero recovers consciousness and immediately jumps up and beats the living day-lights out of the baddie. There's no chance of that sort of thing happening in real life I'm afraid.

As well as working together at the race school, *Chas & Clive* became equal partners in a racing motorcycle spares and parts supply business called Racing Lines. Chas had always been something of a wheeler-dealer throughout his racing career, and he and Clive always got on very well together. We also admired Chas's work ethic. He has never been afraid of work and always puts 100 percent effort into whatever he does.

Racing Lines took off very quickly. Clive did most of the work building the business up, so after about 18 months an amicable decision was made for us to buy Chas out. It had been good fun and Chas had taught us a great deal. Racing Lines was based in John Cooper's workshop premises in Derby. John, our hero, continued to be an advisor and something of a mentor. Racing Lines was situated on the second floor of the building, and our customers had to enter via an external stairway, but it worked very well. The racing motorcyclist is generally a pleasure to deal with. Intelligent, for the most part, and usually knowing exactly what he wants. Charge a fair price and it is a straightforward and easy business.

Racing Lines continued to grow and running it was good fun, except for long periods during the winter time when there was very little trade. Racing is seasonal and finances could get tight to the point of being uncomfortable between clock changes. We went on a few holidays during this time, to places like Cyprus and Florida, picking up good deals because these destinations were quiet in November too. The weather was a bit iffy sometimes but we had no complaints. Hey, we were having holidays. Things were on the up!

The odd waif and stray from the racing world would pitch up at the workshop. One such was a young lad from South Africa called Geoff Larney who worked for us for a while. Geoff was living with the Randles in their White House, and commuting back and forth.

A nicely bought up young man with excellent manners, Geoff had been sent to the UK by his dad to attend 'finishing school'. He polished his racing techniques at Chas's school, raced a season on the British circuits, and generally widened his horizons. His van, one of those little 'sooty van' efforts so popular in South Africa, was exported by ship, from Durban to Southampton with his bike inside. The vehicle came in on a temporary import licence.

One of Ruth's daughters took a fancy to Geoff and this could only mean trouble! Both Chas and Clive had warned him that taking her out was one thing, but falling in love quite another. Do NOT fall in love with her or you'll get hurt. So what did he do? Correct, absolutely head over heels. At the race season's end he returned to South Africa, reluctantly leaving her behind. Of course, when he returned the following March, she had replaced him and he was stunned and utterly heart-broken. See first chapter for more on this painful toughening process. Another example of altered molecular structures hardened by heating and rapid cooling, but still no visible steam!

During his second year in the UK, Geoff was working on his bike in the Racing Lines workshop when a pair of burly besuited bods from Her Majesty's Revenue and Customs descended upon him. These

HMRC gangsters wanted the keys to his van, which was parked outside with its Jo'burg plates still on it. We had all forgotten it was only in the country on a temporary import licence. Geoff just didn't have the cash they demanded so there was nothing we could do, and they took it away until duty was paid at an extortionate and largely arbitrary rate set by them. Despite poor old Geoff being upset, watching those great big men squash themselves into that little van made us all smile, especially because of the sticker on the back window which read: 'We are muff divers, we dive at five'.

John Cooper, that wonderful man, came to Geoff's rescue. John had a contact in the customs business and he managed to negotiate the price down to a more manageable figure, so Geoff could afford to get his van back.

Several years later we spent one of our winter holidays in South Africa and we visited Geoff at his home near Johannesburg. A grown man by then, running his dad's factory and full of confidence, he was married with two daughters. And still a motorcycle racer at heart, he had a couple of bikes in his garage. On first meeting him we knew he would be a success. He had that extra something, and attending finishing school with us did him no lasting damage.

At the same time we were lending our shop 250 Yamaha to Andy Godber, a young farmhand who occasionally came in stinking of silage. He couldn't smell it, of course, as he was totally used to the stuff. Here was a young man the British school system let down very badly. Andy was not at all well schooled, but he was a very intelligent individual who made progress in adult life in spite of the system, not because of it.

Andy was a bit raw and a bit of a loner and we took him under our wing and helped him along. We went all round Europe with Andy and helped him do his carnets and dealing with customs and travelling in East Germany and all that. He won a £1,000 club championship at Donington Park and we went with him to the prize-giving evening, which was great. I took him shopping for his suit, dressed him up in a shirt and tie, and we were both really proud and pleased for him when he got his trophy and his cheque.

He had many other successes too, and later, when he retired from racing, he started his own business and qualified for a pilot's licence. He flew ultralight aircraft, having built his own plane, and he built some for other people too. Britain's education system had overlooked a diamond. If only he had been inspired at school, the system could claim a little credit for some of his achievements. What's more he's turned into a super human being as well. What a great bloke.

Clive finished racing in the most anticlimactic way possible. He was competing in a round of the European Championship at Donington Park, and about halfway through the race he just pulled in, rode into his pit box, flipped up his visor and said he was fed up. That was it! No champagne, no trumpets, no tears, no gnashing of teeth, no drama. He had quit.

It is strange that the ending of the hopes and dreams of a one-time would-be world champion can be so undramatic. It was not what I imagined. He realised he was no longer interested in reducing his lap times. Going faster and faster is the main driving force for a rider, and once no longer driven to do that, it all seemed rather pointless. He was happy about quitting and so was I, I guess. The two people most put out by it were his mum and dad, Ivy and Reg. They would have empty weekends to fill from then on.

Never mind. As Hamlet said: 'There are more things in life, heaven and Earth Horatio than are dreamt of in your philosophy.' Or something like that!

Racing wasn't quite over. We had a family holiday in Daytona where we raced the company's 250cc Yamaha. It was only for fun though, and we took it as an opportunity to have a holiday on the firm, tax deductible. The children were big enough to enjoy Orlando and all the parks, and we all had a lovely time as you might expect. The bike seized its crankshaft in the race and, rightly or wrongly, PJ1 oil was blamed. But how could that possibly be? Kenny Roberts advertised it on the side of his fairing. Aha, that's as may be, but he used Castrol 747 in his bikes we later came to understand. I have mentioned Clive's naivety before, have I not.

I loved the buzz of a race meeting and since Clive retired I've really missed it, although we were back in the paddock for a while looking after Andy and with Racing Lines, of which more anon.

A lot of our money over the years went on racing but I never resented it at all. We still had quite a comfortable home life, and a happy home. Yes, we had to make do with a van rather than have a nice car but that didn't bother me one bit. It was madness but I was happy to join in, and the alternative would have been to sit at home on my own which would have been no good at all. If I'd done that we wouldn't still be together now.

There were some wives and girlfriends that didn't have the same attitude, but those are the ones that have long since gone. When I came into Clive's life he was already racing and I wanted to be part of it. It never occurred to me for a second that I should try to change him or stop him from doing it. In fact, I actually really enjoyed the life. It was very exciting.

Even in the early days, because Clive had three jobs and I was working too we usually had a little spare cash and we could afford the occasional treat. We didn't have credit cards in those days of course, so we just had whatever we carried in our pockets. I didn't mind roughing it and sleeping in the back of the van. At least we got to sleep together.

Cooking and catering was difficult but I just got on with it and did what had to be done. I was required to perform a minor miracle every weekend and I like to think I rose to the challenge. We didn't have the money to go out and find a restaurant or use the paddock cafe for every meal so there was no choice in the matter. Jobs just had to be done, and my attitude was to get on with it and do the best I can. It was better for us all if I made a decent bed and cooked a good lunch. It made for a better atmosphere and made things run more smoothly.

And we needed that calmness. For a rider to be on the top of their game, he needs a stable base. Normal things have to carry on happening. I was always looking forward - what's coming next? Right, I'll get ready for that so when the time comes it's done. The way I saw it, I had a job which had to be taken every bit as seriously as the racing part of the weekend, albeit in the background.

Racing Lines (GB) Ltd

R acing lines GB Ltd went from strength to strength, and through the success of the business we enjoyed a steady living once again. It was probably something around the national average, nothing more that's for sure, but family life did have a less chaotic rhythm and we were content with our lot.

Clive was working all hours, but our relationship remained as strong as ever. Clive had always encouraged me to try to stop smoking, I understand why. It was becoming a costly business, and it is not good for one's health, but I enjoyed it and it was my only vice, so there! But he never let up and one day I casually said I would quit if he made me pregnant once again. I should note at this point I have never smoked while pregnant. It seems unfair to make a baby absorb toxins when it has no choice in the matter.

Well, he didn't need telling twice and straight away we were doing everything possible to have a baby. 'By jove!' I thought at one point, gripping the edges of the wobbling dining table, hoping that the legs, held only by screws and wing nuts would not give way, 'He does seem keen for me to quit smoking!'

My desire for another baby does, on the face of it, seem rather selfish as we had two, lovely, perfectly healthy children already, but I had miscarried a full-term baby named Ben the previous year, and you never completely get over an experience like that. Ever. It is devastating, and you are always wondering what you did wrong, whether you were at fault. Was I negligent in some way? Or was it just an act of God? Either way, it is very difficult to deal with.

Once baby Adam was born, I considered my period of abstinence was over and went out and bought a packet of 20 Benson & Hedges.

But when Clive saw me smoking again he went berserk, snatched the packet from my hand, and jumped up and down on it, behaving like Rumpelstiltskin when the princess speaks his name! He felt betrayed, and said that he had assumed it would be forever. I, on the other hand, had only meant it to be for the duration of the pregnancy. An unfortunate misunderstanding. He swore he would never do another deal without getting a solicitor involved, that he should have got me to sign a contract. Oh well, another bumpy life experience to get over.

Shortly after this we moved house. We left our three-up, three-down, centrally-heated semi that cost a tenner a week in mortgage payments, for a two-up, two-down house heated only by a single coal fire. It got worse. There were no electric lights, and the shower room was outside in what we laughingly called the extension. This was, in fact, two ex-British Rail goods wagons knocked into one space, and only loosely attached to the house. This palatial accommodation cost us ten times as much as our old place. Oh what had we done?

The thing is, we loved it. The house was well off the road and standing in an acre of ground. In the estate agent's blurb it was described as a smallholding, and in former years it had been a coal yard, a haulage yard and a pig farm. Coincidentally, it was sold to us by Clive's mum's bridesmaid, so it felt a bit like destiny. All that space for three children to play in. For us at that point in time it was perfect.

I don't mean that literally, of course. It was far from perfect in very many ways, but with masses of hard work we knew we could make it something special, and while we pulled it round the kids had a fantastic adventure playground. But although we knew it could be perfect and the kids had a ball, it was a veritable hell-hole for me. The shower backed up and could take half a day to drain, and I had to get up at 5am in the winter to light a coal fire to take the frost off the rooms. Clive did all the manly stuff outside, chopping wood and felling the odd tree. He started with a heavyweight, two-handed felling axe, but soon gave up, collapsing with exhaustion. It is absolutely draining work and nothing like you see on the movies. Exit lumberjack stage left!

Next Clive demolished and removed the concrete section air raid shelter that had been home to the 1940s bridesmaid's goat. She kept pigs too, but they were all gone now, and only a couple of horses and two vicious Shetland ponies were about the place. Oh yes they were vicious alright. Hard to believe, but they were a nasty pair of devils. Once they were taken away we started landscaping and the field was turned into a lawn, with help from wonder boy Andy Godber and his farming connections. Clive also built for the kids something we came to call the Death Slide. A terrifying zip-line that started from a point well over 25 feet high in one of our trees, and spanned a distance of more than 50 yards to another. The launch platform was built out of scaffolding planks and stood at the triangulation of the tree and a couple of telegraph poles buried in the ground. All rather dangerous if you'd ask me, and some sensible visiting children were too scared to use it. After first trying, and failing, to utilise the foot pegs that came fixed to the telegraph poles, access was by ladder.

The Horton Death Slide kept the testosterone-infused, the heroic, and the dimwitted and simply daft entertained for years, fortunately without major incident. Oh, apart from the day one of Dan's friends came to tell me he was dead! He had fallen from the platform and landed on his face, broken his collarbone and knocked himself out. I was on my own that day while that husband of mine was enjoying life somewhere else, the b*****d!

The Movies

We ran Racing lines for more than 20 years, with plenty of ups and downs. There were a great many ups but one of the first major downs (for me, at least) started in 1987 when Clive received a phone call out of the blue from Chas. At that time Chas was running a Racing Team using 500cc three-cylinder two-stroke Hondas. Very expensive bikes to run, but beautiful machines. One of the riders was an Italian while the other was British former works Honda starlet Roger Hairnet (actually Burnett, of course). The mechanics were a quiet, fastidious Japanese (is there any other type?) and a rather rough, ready and noisy Italian. The result? Personality clashes and a cold war. Chas wanted Clive to become the peacemaker, or at least try to sort them all out. It went pretty well in all. The mismatched mechanics would never be firm friends, but the ill feeling went away. Clive liked them both and they are still in contact.

All well and good, but problems started for me as result of Clive then getting involved with a film production company which had got in touch with Chas via Kenny Roberts. Kenny was too busy to help them, so they asked Chas to supply a complete racing team that could compete in Grands Prix, but as far as practicable stick to a movie script while doing so. Filming on the movie - working title American Built but eventually called Race for Glory - was due to start at the end of June 1988, and it was now April.

Of course, Chas accepted the job, delegating much of the work to Clive. This work entailed preparing the bikes, painting them and recruiting another mechanic to help. Clive engaged a multilingual Belgian (aren't they all?) called Kamile de Brue. He had been a friend of ours for years and was full of confidence and experience. He was a huge asset.

But I was not all that happy about all this, if I am honest, and with good reason. I discovered I was pregnant yet again! (I was beginning to find out how this was happening by now, too!) Furthermore, the goods wagons (our shed and bathroom) were in the midst of being demolished, and a two-storey brick extension was being built onto the house. It would mean me running Racing Lines too, as Clive would be away with the racing team and film crew for weeks at a time. Of course, he wasn't concerned in the least and why would he be? He was off on his motorcycling travels once again, and he thought he was doing his bit by earning good money. End of conversation!

My list of jobs now consisted of housekeeper, wife, business secretary, mother, shop-keeper, building project manager and taxi driver! Emma was training to be a gymnast, spending three evenings a week at a gym in Alfreton, a round trip of eighty miles each time. I was driving a nice new, white Volvo 740 (you remember, the one that looked like a poor man's Cadillac), so at least the journeys were fast and comfortable. Looking back, to keep everything going I should have been snorting some kind of marching powder, definitely not available on the NHS. Having said that, I think I may secretly have enjoyed the pressure. A bit of self flagellation never did anyone any serious harm did it? It was a bit of a nightmare though.

Clive, on the other hand was enjoying life to the full. The cast and crew and the newly-assembled Samurai Racing Team all got along well. Incidentally, one of the actors was a chap called Peter Burg who has since gone on to become a well known director. Look him up on Google! Alex McArthur was the lead, and Kato from the Pink Panther movies was the Japanese factory boss, but not as Kato, obviously!

The two professional riders, Donnie McLeod and Mike Baldwin, seemed to enjoy their roles, at least for the most part. They had quite a task in fact as they had to qualify for the Grands Prix and take part in the races proper. Donny stunt doubled for the 'goodie' in white leathers and Mike was the 'baddie', dressed in black of course, and their works Samurais were painted to match. The entourage went to Spa in Belgium, Rijeka in Yugoslavia, Paul Ricard in France and Donington Park in the UK, Travelling around Europe as part of the Grands Prix, being paid wages, and living on quite reasonable expense accounts, what was there not to like? Lucky so-and-sos!

When the time came for the 'goodie' in the movie to up his game he needed a new machine that looked strikingly different from the other bikes in the field; something eye-catching, something sensational, remarkable, even. But when Kamile saw the art department's sketches he thought they came nowhere near fulfilling the brief. Their proposals looked rather dull, he thought. So Clive had his bike painter sketch a stars and stripes alternative that was absolutely stunning.The film bosses approved the idea, Clive and Kamile built it, and when they brought the finished bike to the race track it received everyone's whole-hearted approval. Everyone loved it. Donny, perhaps, was a little less enthusiastic than the rest as he would be riding it, but what else can you expect from a Scotsman? They are described as dour for a reason.

The acting side of things took place at the circuits on the days immediately following each featured Grand Prix. Several top factory teams and their riders were contracted to take part in controlled action sequences at different parts of the tracks, all of which were carefully designed to fit in with the script.

Filming tends to be all go or all stop. There is much frantic hurrying around and also a lot of waiting around. During these periods it was quite something to see people like Wayne Gardner, Eddie Lawson, Christian Sarron, Kevin Schwantz and many others who, just the day before, had been gladiators in the arena fighting each other to their last breath, now sitting on each other's machines, chatting socially and laughing and joking. Oh what the idle fellows of the motorcycling press missed out on by rushing off home on Sunday nights and failing to take an interest in that project.

The European part of the project concluded in August with filming at the historic banked test track at Montlhery near Paris. Poor old Clive had to stay, all expenses paid, in the Regina Hotel for two weeks. Oh they treated him terribly, poor fellow! He did deign to return for a weekend to accompany me on a hospital visit. The production paid for him to fly British Airways business class to East Midlands airport, just up the road from home.

It was good to have him home, relieving some of the pressure for a day or so, but then he promptly returned to Paris. It felt a bit like having a general flying in to give his infantrymen (me) a pep talk. A little stiffening of the spine, keep calm and carry on sort of thing, then he cleared off back behind the lines before the fighting started again. He was scoring very few points with me during this period I don't mind telling you. Ah well, it's all water under the bridge now. Time is a great healer, if you allow it to do its work.

Right Stunt

W hen all this lovin' life and livin' it to the full finally came to an end, Clive returned home to family life and his pregnant wife, and to a race shop that needed to be run. But, being the professional that he was (or perhaps the frustrated performer?), he had sat down and read the movie script from front to back. In doing this he had worked out that only the second half of the film had been filmed, and that in the first half of the story there was more motorcycling action which as yet had not been shot. He volunteered himself for two further weeks' work in Boston, USA to look after the bikes and do some stunt riding, and his offer was accepted!

Well, he was leaving me in the lurch once again, and I was as cross as hell! I was up to my neck in family and work stuff while he was living it up once more. I had to concede he would be earning good money, but I argued against the plan nonetheless. Of course, Clive would have none of it. He was enjoying himself far too much, and so enamoured with it all was he, that after a while no further discussion would be entertained. He now believed he had become indispensable as a motorcycling consultant to the Hollywood film industry!

I drove him to Heathrow in our Racing Lines van to deliver the crated motorcycles for dispatch to Boston the following day. We did have a pleasant night together in the Sheraton Hotel, and managed to part in fairly good humour in the end. The next day I drove home alone and reflected. Now three months pregnant, I was doing the work of three people while he was swanning off to spend a fortnight in the Sheraton in Boston, Massachusetts. The b*****d!

Clive was in his element. Folks were asking for his autograph, people wanted locks of hair and to touch his garment. He felt like Mick Jagger. OK, I may be exaggerating just a bit, but he was mixing with actors and actresses and having a ball, which, I'm afraid to say, cheesed me off a bit. Acting types were always getting divorced! I didn't trust them, it was as simple as that. I trusted him... at least I thought I did. But what if he was lured? What if he was tempted by someone with similar luring talents to me? I felt rather uncomfortable if I'm honest. What the eye can't see the mind fabricates, and the torture can be terrible.

He returned on time, having had the time of his life, and with a right few quid in the bank too which did mollify me a little. I had by now convinced myself he had been up to no good and it poisoned me somewhat, I'm afraid to say. I worked off my anger with frenzied bouts of gardening, having a bit of free time once again now he was taking on some of his professional and domestic duties. But I am afraid the green-eyed monster had unbalanced me a little and had soured our relationship. Our dealings were more professional than those of two that are one, if you understand me.

Then in early December there was a phone call from the movie producers. They needed what are called 'pick up' shots, and they wanted the bikes and Clive, to fly back to the States for another filming session, scheduled for the week before Christmas, at a race circuit near Atlanta, Georgia. Was he up for it? Of course he was! Our relationship deteriorated still further. The money was important, I will readily admit. We ran a race shop which could be the world's worst business to own in the middle of winter, but this turn of events was not good for marital harmony.

Clive claimed he was in love with me. Ah yes, but he loved the film business more, is how I saw it. But I put my professional hat on and dealt with the situation the best I could through gritted teeth and with not a few tears of frustration. He returned on schedule full of the joys and dead chuffed with himself, but I could not banish my dark thoughts. Baby Joe was born - no problems - and I had nothing tangible to complain about. Life was good, yet still the green-eyed one would not leave me.

Clive bought me a brand new white Peugeot 205GL. What a huge and delightful surprise to find it on the driveway on the morning of my birthday complete with a love letter and a bunch of flowers on the passenger seat. That should have healed the rift. I should have been in raptures, and in a way I was, but I rather held back. I convinced myself this generosity and thoughtfulness was not simply my reward for being the best wife a bloke could ever want. Perhaps it was because he had indeed been messing about. I had no proof, of course. When you are suffering from jealousy you don't need any. I never said anything to him, I just festered about it… for several years! I still carried out my wifely duties but with little enthusiasm, and I felt devoid of any passion. Clive often talks about duty. In his view it is an important aspect of life. 'Dooty's Dooty, says I' is one of his favourite rejoinders, usually announced in the style of Robert Newton's characterisation of Long John Silver in Treasure Island, often accompanied by an 'Ooh arrgh!'. In our long relationship I have only very occasionally failed in my duty.

Clive sold the Volvo 740 and replaced it with a Toyota MR2 sports car in fire engine red. Not exactly a family car, but we had my little Peugeot for family stuff, he thought. How he worked out the mental arithmetic for that one I know not. There were six members of our immediate family now so how on earth were we meant to mobilise ourselves as a group using a two-seater and a small saloon? He realised soon enough his mathematical formula required more work when we needed both cars for a family holiday in the Lake District and Scotland.

We had a two tier family by now with two teenagers and two smaller children, but it was a successful holiday nevertheless. Clive and Emma climbed Scafell Pike and Ben Nevis, Lord alone knows why. We overran Trevor and his wife who had moved north to live in a mud hut in Caithness for some reason. They are probably a bit, well… let's say eccentric. Actually, I have spent most of my life with motorcycle racing people and I have found that while they might appear fine on the outside, they are definitely all cracked on the in. The racing fraternity are all free-roaming lunatics! Yes, there can be no doubt about it! They are all at least a little bit bonkers, and having reached this conclusion, I guess those involved with them can give ourselves a pat on the back for doing our bit for care in the community.

Take 'em down

Racing Lines was basically a pirate company. Ooh arrgh! We imported racing motorcycles and spare parts from manufacturers in various parts of the world, selling them on more cheaply than larger, legitimate enterprises, usually by cutting out the official importers. This was much to some people's chagrin, I suspect, but we were relatively small fry. These importers and official dealers must have had a smile on their faces when we were sued!

We had sold a racing motorcycle to a pair of brothers, one was a rider, the other his mechanic. Early in March, as soon as was possible, they had taken their brand new machine and raced it at Mallory Park. Unfortunately the rider crashed it at very high speed and the bike was extensively damaged. Totally wrecked, actually. You can imagine the devastation these two chaps felt. Their pride and joy, their ten thousand quid's worth of racing motorcycle, and with it all their hopes and dreams lay in a twisted, crumpled heap. Their erstwhile new bike was scrap, most likely. Sifting through the wreckage a few days later they found something they could blame.

In my experience, only rarely will a rider take full responsibility for his own mistakes. Only very, very rarely. He will always endeavour to blame anything but himself. A tyre, another rider, the racing surface, anything but himself. I am using the male term for a rider as they are most usually, with just a few exceptions, men. A few female riders have come to the fore, and some of these have been excellent, but nevertheless the vast majority of racing lunatics are, inevitably, men.

Back to the story. This pair of brothers discovered a broken casting in the suspension. Unusual. Odd. You would never expect it. But hang on a minute, this motorcycle had been designed to be raced, not built to survive being crashed at high speed, although race bikes inevitably are crashed, repaired, and then then raced again ad infinitum. They decided to sue the importer, Racing Lines, under the faulty goods act. But Racing Lines was not insured for faulty goods as we had reasoned that we didn't manufacture anything. It was a depressing time. We felt vulnerable and besieged, fighting off these men and their leech-like lawyers by employing our own legal team, at over one hundred pounds an hour! Racing Lines only just managed to pay Clive at an hourly rate of £10 and me at a little less, so you can see how stressful this all was, how utterly depressing and mentally corrosive. It did not do our fragile relationship any good I can tell you.

After a couple of years using our lawyer to bat back legal correspondence from this pair, and after giving serious consideration to the idea of employing a hit man, we decided Racing Lines would go on the attack. Actually, taking the b******s out like in the movies would have been much cheaper as well as being more satisfying. We were told it would only cost a very reasonable four thousand quid! Our approach changed following advice from a friend and colleague with contacts in corporate law. He gave us the name of a chap who had a degree in that subject and also a degree in engineering! Can you conceive of someone having a brain like that?

Once the fightback started, boy was it expensive, but somehow it was less stressful. On the front foot, less scared of the bowler to use a cricketing metaphor, was a far better place to be. By the by, Clive and I have, over the years, gradually become cricket fans. We have watched a few matches at Newlands in Cape Town, and nowadays Clive even prefers a test match on TV to an afternoon watching British Superbikes.

We had a witness who had seen the actual crash. He had been in the race, sitting behind the rider in question at the time. He came into the shop one day and said the plaintiff had gone into the corner too fast, and on cold tyres. The crash had taken place at the first left-hander on the first lap, and this is one of the most common causes of racing accidents. Most tracks run clockwise and the left-side of the tyre takes longer to heat up. Unfortunately, however, our racer witness was reluctant to give evidence. It is hard to believe a motorcycle racer can ever be 'chicken', but sadly this is often the case. They generally do not like direct confrontation, preferring instead to use their racing motorcycles as go-betweens. Face to face, or mano-a-mano, they often have difficulty.

We built a technical defence based on mathematics, motorcycle design and technology, metallurgical analysis, and chemistry, and presented it to the plaintiff's lawyers, who, after due examination, and having discovered they had contrived to lose their evidence in the interim, capitulated and withdrew. We were then able to counter-claim for our expenses. Our costs were over eight thousand pounds, a figure reached without any value being placed on the stress, strain and depression we had been through. Lawyers never suffer in this way, of course, so they don't understand the concept. Each case is just part of life's rich tapestry to them.

So all we wanted was our money back. Fairly straightforward, you would think, but oh no! A moderator gets involved and chips the claim down until you get only around half in actual cash terms. I can understand this concept, and the need for it. Your lawyer may have taken luncheon at the Ritz every day and claimed it as an unavoidable expense, so there have to be checks. The moderator makes sure the system is not abused, but in our case also that injustice remains a pillar of the British legal system. We won our case but ended up nearly four thousand quid out of pocket! Justice? Is there such a concept?

As a result of this draining experience we endeavoured to get some insurance cover for this kind of thing. What a good idea it turned out to be as we were sued again. This time because a wheel collapsed under a well-known rider at the TT. At that time we were importers for the Italian manufacturers of the component. It was a big deal, massive actually, and the rider was injured very badly too.

We coped better with the court case this time as we had an insurance company in our corner, but going to court was a whole new experience, especially as the venue was the High Court in London. The Old Bailey is a most impressive building, intimidating in fact. Fortunately, our case was being heard in a shed around the back! OK, not quite a shed, more a large office with a raised dais for the judge so it was slightly less unnerving than it might have been, although it was a very serious business with a proper judge very firmly in control of the room.

The Italian firm was also being sued; severally and liable is the term, I believe. When the Italians entered the court wearing big dark coats like the Mafia in a movie some light comedy was introduced, and this increased when their QC started to speak with a stammer. Surely the last thing a QC needs is a speech impediment, you would think. Now you have to admire the fellow and I do not in any way want to denigrate folk with this affliction, but it was not the job for him. Like an agoraphobe being a ploughman, or an aquaphobe working as a life guard. Doable, but why make life hell for yourself?

The judge was marvellous and saw through any attempt at embroidery or deceit. He made a mockery of some of the flimsier evidence and dodgy witness statements given in his court. All very candid and to the point, and we have great respect for judges on the whole. Nevertheless, our side lost.

Amazingly the wheel manufacturers had no insurance, quite staggering in modern times. And how an Italian company managed to run a manufacturing process like a foundry without the usual national government nose-bagging is another small wonder. As a consequence our insurance company was left holding the baby, as it were. It paid all the plaintiff's costs and the rider's damages as well, and he *was* damaged too, of that there was never any doubt.

No money was forthcoming from the wheel manufacturers whose entire responsibility it was, and there was no chance of any without further legal process through the Italian courts. I don't know what the final upshot was, although the affair cost Racing Lines a further three and a half thousand pounds thanks to a bit of wriggling and squirming from our insurance company. You pay the premiums and think you are on a ladder, or are at least safe from snakes, but there is always one you slide down somewhere. I think most people expect that kind of thing from insurance firms.

In conclusion, if you ever go to court don't lie to the Judge. That would be my rule number one. Other lessons learned were that if you lose it's expensive, and if you win it costs plenty too. The b******s!

207

New Millennium

A round the turn of the millennium we were beginning to lose interest in Racing Lines. The sport was slowly but surely going over to road bike-based four-strokes, yet the costs for competitors was rising inexorably. Go figure, as our American friends would say. Compared to purpose-built racing machines, modified road bikes made in their millions should be much cheaper to buy and race, not more expensive!

We refocused by securing a contract with Dunlop to be tyre supplier and service agent for a new championship series run by MRO (Motorcycle Racing Organisation). The series was intended to be a stepping stone for competitors aiming to compete in the British Championships. We always got on well with the people at Fort Dunlop, particularly a stalwart employee there called Phil Plater. Phil was an honest guy who carried authority easily, yet could still relate to the regular guy. When Dunlop all but wound up and Phil took early retirement it was a doubly sad loss for the sport in our view.

This contract required us to buy a 7.5 ton van and all the tyre changing kit and accoutrements needed to do a professional job in the paddock, and while Clive wrestled with the wheels and tyres, I was the head of wheel balancing and looked after the accounts (and debt collection!). We'd set off on a Friday evening loaded to the gunwales, and then upon arrival at Brands Hatch or Cadwell Park or wherever, we'd put up a huge awning and unload the heavy tyre machine. We'd be up and working straight away and hardly stop until the end of the meeting on Sunday afternoon, by which time we would usually be physically shattered. There were several meetings where we sold and changed over 100 tyres, making a fiver each time, but then again there was one weekend when we only sold one, so it wasn't always beer and skittles. Still, we loved the pressure, and the fact it was good, old fashioned work. It keeps you fit and feeling wholesome. There is nothing to compare to it.

But the tyre business is a dirty one and things got difficult when competitors started to get hold of the same tyres for less than we could buy them for directly from Dunlop. How crazy is that? As time went on things became heated and we had to to sue a former friend and competitor in the small claims court for non-payment of an invoice. All rather crumby and disappointing. Some people!

In the end we were happy to get out of the motorcycle racing spares business altogether, and in 2005 we sold Racing Lines to an ambitious and hard-working young man called Rob Mawbey. Clive pretty much retired at that point, but Rob asked me to stay on for a while to help him find his feet. It was only supposed to be for a couple of months but it's been over ten years now and I'm still helping out part-time. We've been through thick and thin, Rob and I. The business used to be road racing-oriented, because that's what Clive knew, but now we do quite a bit of road bike stuff, as well as motocross, quads and much else.

Clive and I did not miss the mental stress of running a business, but we did both miss the people and the buzz of the MRO paddock. We missed the fun and laughter with friends, and the fact we could no longer offer our advice and support to the competitors, some of whom would later move onwards and upwards to GP level. Casey Stoner and Cal Crutchlow to name only two. But back then those two young men and most of their rivals did not take themselves too super-seriously, and the sport could still be enjoyed as it should.

Clive took on a part-time coaching appointment with the ACU for a couple of years, and I would often accompany him. You can't let a diabetic run free in the wild without his carer on stand-by can you?

He threw himself into the job and derived a great deal of pleasure from it, and he also enjoyed working for the the Ron Haslam Race School at Donington Park.

Clive worked there as a briefer, which involved talking the pupils through the track rules and procedures at the start of the day, and then debriefing them and giving them a report and certificate at the end. He used to try to have a bit of banter with the pupils, and make them laugh if he could. He has always said if people are laughing they're learning a lot more and little nuggets of information stick.

Ron is a famous ex-racer, of course, and he is the figurehead of the school. But his wife Ann runs it. She is the captain of the ship and don't you forget it! Ann is a formidable person and not to be messed with. One day Ann told Clive she needed someone to take charge of the kit room at the school, and she wondered if I might be interested in the job. I gave her a ring and she invited me over for a chat. That was 14 years ago and I've been working for her ever since.

A few of the pupils are would-be racers but the majority are ordinary motorcyclists who want to see what it's like on the track from a racer's perspective. Many have been bought the experience as a gift from wives or children, often to mark a significant birthday. Clive says a lot of the older guys get given a day at the school by wives hoping to see the back of them!

In the kit room we have to sort the guys (and girls) up with leathers, gloves, boots and helmets. The school can supply a full kit if necessary and it's my particular job to make sure everything fits as it should and that they know what they're doing, and then we send them off on their way.

We're the first people they see after they've signed on and they're all very, very nervous, and we try to make them feel welcome and settle them down. Sometimes because you kit someone up in the morning they keep coming back for advice or just to chat, and you end up looking after them all day, which is no trouble at all. It's a pleasure.

We had one guy who was dying of cancer and did not have long to go, which was quite moving, and I had a German guy who was there the whole day completely on his own. He was very lost and extremely nervous and at the end of the day he came to see me, put his hand on my arm and said, 'You have made me feel very safe today.' It was really heartfelt and it almost made me cry. Then he padded off again in his Y-fronts. Corporate guests are not so much fun. They tend to think they're it, somehow above everybody else and that the school's rules don't apply to them.

I must say all the pupils are superbly looked after by the instructors, many of which are top BSB riders such as James Westmoreland and Michael Rutter. Both nice guys, but there are one or two well-known riders who can't even be bothered to say hello to you. Can't be seen speaking to a kit room girl, oh goodness me no!

The classic racing scene has been booming in recent years and Clive's done a bit of parading, but nostalgia's not really for him. He says he's not bothered about watching has beens. If someone asks him to ride their bike he might do it out of politeness, but he'd just rather not because he says going round several seconds a lap slower than he could at his peak is frustrating beyond all belief. That makes sense really, because for Clive lap times meant everything. When he came in after a race, no matter where he finished, the first thing he'd say was: 'What was my lap time?'

Actually, some of the parading can be quite fast but he knows he can't get near his old times so he'd rather not bother. He says he's not competitive any more, but actually he is. It's just that he'd get frustrated. To stay fast you've got to keep doing it. Ron Haslam is still quick but he's never really stopped riding. He's got a 140mph brain now and he used to have a 200mph brain, whereas Clive's only got a 60mph brain these days.

I'm a bit nostalgic about the old days but Clive's attitude is the past has gone and there's no point living there. He's thrown a lot of his old trophies and plaques away, even the Grand Prix ones. There isn't a display cabinet at home with them all in. We've kept a few, the ones that mean the most. Clive says he gets sick of them. They get rusty and tarnished anyway, and every now and again he has a clear-out and a few more go to the tip. I think he's gone a bit too far, to be honest. All racing trophies are so hard-earned whatever the level of competition and no matter what bike you're on, but that's his way. We don't even keep all the TT replicas together. Daniel's got one and Clive's brother another.

We went to a big classic event at Mallory Park a couple of years ago and I really enjoyed it. It was great to see Clive back in leathers and he looked as happy as Larry until he got out on the track for practice. The conditions were wet and filthy and the bike was horrible. An air-cooled, cable disc-braked Honda MT125, the same as he'd won the Honda championship on. He said he thought, 'How the hell did I get one of these around here as fast as I did?'

But he did enjoy the technical input, being able to tell the owner how to set the bike up and that it was over-geared. His old rival Rod Skivyer was the mechanic on it and he understood Clive's long list of jobs to do on the bike and got stuck in. But Clive never went out again to test the improvements. He got a kidney stone and had to be carried off to the medical centre. He was in agony and one of the guys carting him off kept making him laugh and of course that made it hurt more and more. Anyway, he was heavily drugged up to kill the pain so that was it as far as going out on the track was concerned. We went home early which was a shame but Clive wasn't too bothered. 'I don't need to prove I can't do it any more,' he said. 'I know I can't.'

Clive calls classic festivals old duffers' events. Phil Read will be at these meetings and he is still being Phil Read. Still being that swaggering, confident dude who was a bit of a rebel and won eight world championships. Clive loves Phil and still admires him greatly, but his own attitude is that was then and this is now. 'I loved it, marvellous, what a privilege, but I don't want to relive it, thanks.' But as for me, I'm still involved in motorcycling quite a bit by working for Rob at Racing Lines and for the Haslams at the race school; and I watch MotoGP and British Superbikes most weekends while Clive prefers watching cricket these days! I guess bikes are in my blood and that's it.

Back on track

Clive and I get on really well again now, and our relationship started out on the road to recovery with a summer road trip to Paris. Imagine this: an offer of a romantic weekend in Paris after being driven there in a red sports car with the roof down. I can't say I was too bothered at first, if I'm honest. But Clive was making a big effort to win me over, so I thought what the heck, let's do it.

After eight hours on the road we were in our hotel, a cheap one close to the Montmartre, with sunburned foreheads! Open-topped cars are great in theory, and quite fun in practice, but if you've got one, don't forget to wear a hat! What a lovely ride. The ferry took me back to our days on the continental circus. I enjoyed the drive, and I couldn't have cared less about the sunburn actually. In Paris we walked everywhere and the car stayed in the garage, and we had an altogether lovely time in the city of romance. Clive's plan worked and in the bedroom there was a further thawing out of our relations. We were back to being a complete couple with both parties fully engaged and fulfilled once again.

We saw almost everything tourists in Paris are supposed to, and even got caught in a cloudburst and were soaked through near the Eiffel Tower, running hand in hand with a newspaper over our heads. Oh hang on! That last bit may have been in a movie I've seen. Never mind, I don't care. It was a fabulous romantic break which put our relationship well and truly back on track. We should go back and visit the Musee d'Orsay next time, as it was closed. We have visited many cities since then on further romantic battery-charging breaks. All the following are particularly recommended: Venice, Rome, Prague, Salzburg, Washington and Cape Town. We have been so lucky.

But camping is hardly every girl's dream is it? The rain, the mud, the squalor, the creepy-crawlies - always something to dread? Not in Kruger Park in South Africa, it's lovely, so said Clive as this was another of his crazy ideas. Camping and hiking in a place filled with lions, hyenas, poisonous spiders, snakes, elephants, giraffes, rhinos, hippos, wildebeests etc. Oh yeah, what could possibly go wrong! Oh well, banking on it maybe being fun after all, we gave it a go, and we two and the two younger boys had a camping holiday and a walking safari. It was great actually, as we learned quite a bit. For example we were taught to differentiate between hyena, elephant and rhino dung, all of which Clive threw at the children for amusement. In camp, the toilet facilities were extra special. At the rear of the tent was mounted a wooden deck on which one could shower, shave and share the wilderness. Sitting on the porcelain throne while hearing lions roar - what an unforgettable privilege!

And camping wasn't the end of it. Camping is for sissies. No, we stayed a night in a Zulu camp, in a rondavel: a traditional native hut made of sticks and grass, with no running water or electricity. Actually, we had a posh rondavel with a proper toilet so I can't complain. We ate with the Zulus in a big wooden shed (another concession for the visitors), and at dinner time when we stepped outside our torchlit hut we had never seen blackness so black! There were no street lights, of course, and that night there was no moon either, Blimey! How on earth were we meant to find the eating shed?

Knowing his visitors were helpless, the village chief sent us a guide. What a nice man. He sent us a child who held our hands and led us through the darkness. The food was pretty authentic, I would say, although it was hard to tell exactly what it was by candle-light. The meal was followed by dancing, drumming and stamping. Zulu stamping is turbo-charged. The knee is raised high, then the foot is hammered into the floor and no effort is spared. When there is a bunch of those guys doing it on a dirt floor the sound is thunderous, and the smell of these smoky, sweaty, black bodies was all rather stimulating. When we left this Zulu camp we went for an overnight stay in another one that was a bit more up my street, if I'm honest. More of a Disney Zulu-land than the real thing, it was actually the film set built for the movie Shaka Zulu, and it had been turned into a theme motel called Shaka Land. One had a native chap to carry one's bags from the car to reception. This local chappie, wearing nothing but a loin cloth, led us in his bare feet along a gravel path. If Clive had swapped places with him, he would have shouted 'Ow,Ow,Ow' with every step, and upon reaching reception he would have wept and handed in his notice.

At Shaka Land visitors can volunteer to fight a gnarly old Zulu using sticks! Clive did this and took a humiliating beating. You can also have a bash at throwing an assagai or umkhontou (a spear). Young Zulus threw them into a wooden fence about 30 yards away, into which they stuck, quivering, about eight feet up. Clive took them on, in good spirit it must be said, but despite a Fred Trueman-style run up, his umkhontou barely reached the wall. I liked Sharka Land, as did we all, and we left respecting the Zulu a great deal.

Actually, the real reason we went on holiday to QuaZulu-Natal was our shared interest in history. We wanted to visit battle sites. Yes, I know it sounds all rather boring, and it can be just that sometimes, there's no doubt about it, but it can also be fascinating, and it is the unexpected extras that make it really interesting. Listening to our tour guide David Rattray give his account of the battle of Rorke's Drift was simply magical. His soothing, educated, South African accent leaves one quite hypnotised, even though he was speaking of a night battle and describing flames ripping across the burning thatch of a hospital roof. Around four thousand maddened Zulus, desperate to blood their assegais, were beaten back by just one hundred and twenty-nine defenders. I can hear his voice even now saying '…thirty-six of whom were so ill, they were immobile'.

Alas, his knowledge and story-telling skills are now lost. He was murdered a few years later by a Zulu, one of the very people he loved, during a robbery at his guest ranch and nature reserve. Fugitives Drift was a lovely place with a view over a river and the African veldt beyond it to Isandlwana, a modest mountain under which, on the morning preceding the battle of Rourke's Drift (22 January, 1879) the British army was humiliatingly beaten by '…a bunch of savages waving sticks'.

Isandlwana is a place with great atmosphere. Large cairns of stones mark where the bodies of the soldiers are buried in groups where they fell, as they were overwhelmed by the Zulu hoard. The whole story was a delight to listen to, even though we are talking of the deaths of thousands of men. The global politics, the overconfidence of the British, the deception, and the tales of heroism and endeavour altogether weave a story that somehow makes you thankful.

Spion Kop was another battle site we visited. It is marked by the graves of many hundreds who were massacred there in January 1900 during the Boer War. Welcome to the new century lads! The views over the veldt are magical from this hill, although it was a beauty wasted on the unseeing eyes of the poor blighters who were slaughtered in that action, and who now lie under yet more stone cairns. Not far from here was an interesting hotel in a national park at the foot of the Drakensburg mountains. It was visited by the young Princess Elizabeth in 1946 some six or seven years before she became Queen. This is a fact visitors were not allowed to forget, and they even had the car in which she travelled, permanently on show on the front porch. It was all a bit snobbish I have to say, but we rather liked it. Here we stayed in a rondavel-style cabin which was built in brick as accommodation for the cast and crew of the movie Zulu in 1966. This hotel is now closed, and that seems a shame. Whether due to insufficient customers numbers, or because it was trapped in a time warp, or maybe because some natives started robbing hikers in the park, it's hard to know.

There are some upsides to being married to a loon, if you look hard enough. One of these is having a greater than average number of memorable experiences. Oh, how lovely! We are off to the seaside. Durban, to be specific, on the Indian Ocean. Clive had arranged for us to stay in a friend's bungalow there on a golf course. This was all sounding jolly nice, but when we got there, there was no bedding. We should have brought our own, it appeared, and the place had been closed up for several months and green mould was showing here and there. No surprise really as the climate was very humid. It was late at night and I was tired. 'I can't stay here,' I said. 'Our two boys certainly can't stay here, and I am not at all happy.' 'Oh it'll be alright,' said Clive, trying to persuade me to change my mind. But the lady was not for turning and I convinced him we should try the Blue Marlin, a hotel we had passed on the way, and not too distant.

It was a brightly-lit place, but it was late and the front door was locked. I stayed in the car and sent Clive to explore. He returned after five minutes, saying that we were in luck, but would have to go in the back way, through a casino full of desperate-looking hookers and gamblers. 'Just try to avoid looking any of them in the eye.' he said. 'I have spoken to the old bag behind the caged-off bit, where you cash in your chips and she says there is a big four-bed room available, and we can easily afford it too, but we can't have it for another half an hour until its regular occupant has finished with her last client.' I was stunned. Then he smiled, and I knew he was telling one of his embroidered stories, giving himself a bit of a laugh. What a pity no one else laughs at his jokes, he could earn a good living. The b*****d!

Twice! Why twice?

On another holiday in Africa, Clive took Adam and Daniel, our two oldest boys (mid teens and mid twenties at the time) on another camping trip - goodness knows why, he hates camping - and for some crazy reason they decided to climb Kilimanjaro up the Machame route. Madness! Dan had to turn back with altitude sickness, but Adam and Clive made it to the summit. It was a tough ten-day slog, and a massive emotional achievement.

A couple of years after this, I asked a simple question, but in doing so made a huge tactical error. 'What should we do for a holiday this year?' I said. 'Climb Kilimanjaro again.' was the answer. Why anyone would want to do it a second time is beyond comprehension. Perhaps it is something to do with the peculiar nature of the circuit racer's brain?

Racers are constantly searching for the perfect lap, the lap where, on the very edge of disaster, everything is done to the absolute limit of their ability. The throttle is opened at the perfect moment to bring about maximum corner exit speed, the brakes are applied at the last possible moment so as not to waste a microsecond. Perfection is achieved occasionally, if only once every blue moon, but it was rare for Clive to be happy with his performance. He was always thinking he could have done better, even if he won. Winning races was secondary to this striving for perfection.

The nature of racing allows the perfectionist to indulge himself again and again. He can keep building lap after lap in an effort to make the next one a personal best, or even a record breaker. The number of chances he gets is dependent on how may laps the race is, of course. At the TT, with its near forty mile lap, Clive had to wait around twenty minutes, to modify any slight error he may have made. I would guess no rider has ever completed a lap around there and thought to himself: 'Done it - I'm happy now.' I'm sure 'Not bad. Quite good I suppose,' is more likely the thinking.

Regarding climbing Kilimanjaro, most folk would be happy to have done it, but not a racer, or at least not my one. Clive always thinks everything he does lacks a little something. A bit of joy, a soupçon of delight. Upon reaching the summit with Adam, even though there is insufficient air at that altitude to do much more than function on minimum, he wanted to feel more. Had he got to the top and knocked off ninety-nine push ups, I feel sure he would have said: 'I should have done a hundred, I left one up there.'

I was a bit scared if I am honest, but I decided to give it a good go, if only for Clive's sake. I dusted off my team Horton hat, and set about getting fit. Every evening for weeks we knocked off a few training miles, and some weekends we knocked off a great many more, until the day came when we landed at Kilimanjaro International Airport in Tanzania. We were met by our guide, Eligius, a skinny young man, whom I instinctively liked, and who was known to Clive from his previous ascent. Eligius dropped us at our hotel in Arusha and said he would return bright and early the next day to start the six day trek. I was still a bit unsure of myself but Eligius, left me with the good feeling we were in safe and competent hands.

Because Clive is such a kind, considerate and lovely man (you may take a moment here to snigger) we had chosen to ascend, via the Marangu route. Sadly it has attracted the derisory epithet, 'Coca Cola route'. It is the most popular way up the mountain as it features primitive fixed wooden huts for sleeping and resting. In other words, no damn tents. Thank goodness!

We started the trek from a car park, which is already at the same height above sea level as the summit of Ben Nevis, and walked steadily through rain forest to the first overnight stop at Mandara Hut. It was quite a distance, but I was doing OK, I thought. It still felt a bit daft nonetheless, and I could find little joy in it. And when I glanced up at the snow-capped summit, it never looked a millimetre closer.

The food was OK, I suppose: basically popcorn, rice and fruit. All reckoned by our guide to be exactly the right fuel for a summit attempt. There was also as much tea as we could cope with. Vital, apparently, to counter altitude sickness. We had a tough night in the wooden A-frame sleeping hut, mainly due to noisy neighbours. The huts accommodated two groups with a dividing panel in between, and we spent the night only centimetres away from some highly over-excited American-Asian students. They did finally fall quiet and we eventually dropped off to sleep.

I awoke feeling more than a little grumpy, and began stomping about, hurling expletives like a frontline infantryman. This is madness, I don't want to be here. Eff-it and blind-it! It is supposed to be my flippin' holiday. Eff-it! I ignored the fact we had a week lying on a Kenyan beach to look forward to after this crackpot adventure was over.

Rather out of character it must be said, Clive talked to me calmly and quietly telling me it would be perfectly OK if I wanted to return to the hotel, swim in the pool, sunbathe and smoke my cigarettes. My first thought was great! What are we waiting for? But then it slowly dawned on me. Racers never quit, not in my experience anyway. 'You won't be coming with me though, will you?' I said. 'No,' he replied, 'I personally would rather die than turn back now.' Flaming typical! So we ate breakfast in a mouse-infested dining shed. Actually, they were quite sweet little rodents as mice go. Little creatures scuttling about in chipmunk-like striped furry coats, snatching up dropped crumbs, and, once human diners had left, scurrying straight up and onto the tables to scavenge any morsels left behind. They were cute, as I have said, but we tucked our trousers into our socks nonetheless!

Motorcycle racers come in all shapes and sizes, and on their day many have a moment when they are riding so well, they are unbeatable, or at least they feel that they are. They may even think they are world class. Hah! But sometimes it is not self-delusion of course, and one in many thousands turns out to be a Mike Hailwood or a Valentino Rossi. But even lesser mortals such as my Clive have days when they feel completely self confident and fully focused.

Before the start of a race all riders are insecure. You might get the odd time, and Clive has experienced it, when he's stepped onto the grid and thought, 'Well, they'll have to go some to beat me today.' He just felt he was going to win. But that's rare. Most times they're all thinking, I'd just like an extra practice just to make sure I can still do the lap times. They all feel the same insecurity, but I think there are just a few, people like Valentino Rossi and Marc Marquez, who feel like that every day. That's the difference between them and regular guys. It's not swagger, it's genuine self belief and authentic positivity from the very core of their inner being.

There's a lot of self-delusion in the paddock. I'm flying today, I've jetted down and I've geared up, and I'm ready to rock and roll. But it's all bullshit. These guys are just puffing themselves up, and a lot of it is just them trying to convince themselves, or it's empty braggadocio. The quiet ones, we found, were generally the ones to watch.

So on Kilimanjaro Clive had his racing persona to fall back on, while I, on the other hand, had nothing similar to draw on. Nonetheless, I was damned if I was going to quit and I put on my now rather threadbare professional hat and plodded onwards and upwards. Damn and blast it! My mood became further depressed and I fell into sullen silence, my chin getting ever closer to the floor.

We stopped for lunch, close by three effigies, made from grass. Eligius explained it was a memorial to porters who had died from frostbite and exposure a few months previously. Crikey! The weather can change dramatically on a mountain. We were above the cloud line, but it wasn't unbearably cold as we were well wrapped up in sweaters, ski jackets, boots, hats and fancy over-trousers. The deceased porters however, poor fellows lower down the human pecking order, had to make do with torn tee shirts, and second-hand boots worn with no socks. The poor souls died trying to help some white tourists tick off a box on a bucket list.

Later that afternoon, after crossing a precarious wooden bridge spanning a crevasse, and with chin now plowing a furrow in the earth, I felt utterly depressed and absolutely at the end of my tether. Clive, meanwhile, was the epitome of perkiness with his charming, devil-may-care, positive mental attitude. The irritating little s**t! Just when I felt I couldn't get any glummer, the group was called to a halt by Eligius, and with the air of a post prandial speaker, he grandly announced: 'I would like to officially congratulate you all, and welcome you to Horombo Hut!'

Blimey, we had made it to nearly four thousand metres! Clive tells me I unfolded like the petals of a flower, straightening my hunched back - which for some time had been reminding him rather frighteningly of his mother-in-law! - and with my shoulders drawn back I walked straight into that camp like Wellington at Waterloo. He was so proud of my metamorphosis, he couldn't quite get over it. To be over halfway to the summit gave my self confidence a hell of a boost, and I began to think more positively from then on.

A little later, while we were eating in the Horombo canteen, the door burst open and a young woman in her early twenties staggered in on wobbly legs and was helped onto a seat. She had just descended from the summit. Crikey! I thought. If a twenty-something comes back looking like that, what will a fifty-something look like? Several minutes later two tough-looking chaps came in, one very much the worse for wear. Folks are all affected differently, it appeared. Strangely, the super fit seem to suffer worst from being at altitude. I had read that somewhere and thought it must be nonsense, but as I watched the human wrecks in the canteen at Horombo I hoped there was some truth in it.

Horombo is the first overnight stop for walkers on the way down. Of course, it's downhill all the way and the air gains in density with every step. The body's performance improves, the mind gets clearer and frame of mind becomes more positive.

The exhausted returnees recovered quite quickly and less than an hour after their arrival they were chatting and moving around like normal humans. That is the key. If you recover fairly quickly after exertion you are making good progress, and I was. Clive was actually having more difficulty than me. He had become very quiet, and was not all that interested in eating - a sure sign of trouble with him even in normal circumstances. I put it down to his diabetes, so I wasn't overly concerned at his less than cheery demeanour.

He picked up quite a bit later on, and after our evening meal we strolled around the camp, and looked down on the clouds, and as dusk fell we watched the twinkling lights of Moshe, a town far below. That was about it for entertainment. We had brought books to read by torchlight but even that was surprisingly tiring. I know!

Let's renew our membership of the mile high club! Exhausting, but the low air pressure added something extra. We did sleep well.

At daybreak Eligius delivered a bowl of water and a bar of soap, warning us not to leave the latter on view, or the big black birds with vicious-looking beaks, that wheeled overhead and patrolled the outer outer edges of the site would flap down steal it. Good grief, they must have iron constitutions if their guts could tolerate something like that. We shared the warm water, although first up got the cleanest of course. These morning ablutions were the only washes available all week. The toilets were a bit primitive too, reminiscent of 1960s race tracks and of the 'long drop' variety. Much too French if you ask me. Ugh! And at night if you crept out of the hut for a pee in the blackness, you were always uncomfortably aware there could be an unseen mouse, poised on its hind legs, ready to nibble your 'exposings', Eek!

We spent two nights at Horombo as there was is an acclimatisation day in between. On that day we ascended a side vent of the Kilimanjaro volcano passing Zebra Rocks before coming back down to camp. Whether it was of any practical benefit to us or just a time filler is hard to say.

The next day, we set off to Kibo Hut, a rest stop for ascenders only, and perched on the mountainside at nearly 5,000 metres. We walked mainly by ourselves, free walking along a well worn path over what climbers call alpine desert. The route was easy to follow and the weather was delightful. We carried only lightweight 'day sacks' holding water, a packed lunch, and - just in case - a set of waterproofs. Our big 15kg rucksacks were hauled along by the long-suffering porters. Poor sods! Although we were alone we were confident our guide could catch us anytime he felt like it, and knew exactly where we were, as he had made this journey at least a hundred times before.

Once at Kibo there was time to relax in preparation for a night departure for the summit. I was doing OK, but my poor 'pardner' was not looking the full shilling if I'm honest. No matter. When you are willing to die to avoid failure, feeling dreadful can be of little concern. We dressed just before midnight - two pairs of socks and extra layers of everything as we were warned it would be bitterly cold. I felt like the Michelin Woman.

After strapping our headlamps over our woolly hats we followed Eligius in line astern with all the discipline of an SAS secret patrol. Except for Clive, that is. There is always one is there not? He kept pulling over for a pee, marking the path like a mountain dog. Clive reckons he knows African ways fairly well, having studied the Anglo Zulu wars extensively. He says, they never call people by their given names, except on formal occasions. Instead, they use nicknames which suit people's personalities, or refer to past incidents in their lives, or comment on their physiology. Perhaps big nose or five bellies for obvious reasons. As for someone who pees every ten minutes, perhaps PissPot?

I felt nauseous at one point and had a bit of a puking session. Altitude has many side effects and I was exhausted too. Some rock climbing was involved, although not enough to need climbing gear or ropes, but it was more than just scrambling. At one point Eligius grabbed my hand and pulled me over a huge boulder, before saying 'Congratulations, you have arrived at Gillman's point!' It was a bit of a non-event to be honest but I smiled grimly. We'd made it to the rim of the crater.

It was still well before sunrise and we posed for flash photographs in front of a weathered sign. I thought it was all over, but it wasn't quite yet. Eligius decided we had time, if Clive would only get off all fours and finish vomiting, to march around the rim and reach the absolute summit of the mountain at Uhuru Peak at just short of six thousand meters. Wow!

Of course the whole point of setting off at midnight had been to watch the sunrise from the very top of the mountain, but I was happy enough to be at Gilman's. More walking was a daft idea, but what the heck, we followed him for another half hour, to the highest point on Kilimanjaro. At Uhuru Peak more photos were taken to commemorate our valiant efforts, only in bright sunlight this time. I was on 'Top of the world, Ma' to borrow a phrase from James Cagney, and I smoked a fag in celebration. And as the sun lit up my life once again I decided every sunrise would be magic from now on! And it has been.

The end

Though not quite......

Epilogue. Written in my absence ...... by Clive

In 2018, at 68, I finally passed my bike test. It's not unusual for a racer to be licenseless and I needed one. I'd rebuilt a pair of Vincents and planned to ride them on the road - even if my instructor had said of my riding "there's much work to do"! It was around this time however that Sue noticed I was losing weight and looking a bit yellow. I won't bore you with the details but ultimately an operation was aborted with Sue receiving a phone call to apologise for the fact that they were unable to remove the cancer. Blimey! That was the first time they'd used the word and Daniel, our eldest and no longer the premature light weight of 40 years ago, but a robust police sergeant, asked "Do we need to save up for a Christmas present or what"? Light relief is just what you need in dark moments and the atmosphere was greatly lifted, but the doctor remained non-committal.

Someone needed to show positivity and leadership and as ever Sue picked up the mantle. I started to shuffle around and ultimately it was a routine diabetes appointment which saw us turn the corner. "Crikey you have been through the wars since we last met!" the doctor said. "You are not kidding, we still don't have a prognosis though". "Well I can tell you!" She obviously had all the now very thick notes in front of her. "You have something called IGG4. It is very rare, it is an auto immune disease". Not cancer at all then? The surgeon must have taken a biopsy when he had me in his workshop. The NHS is absolutely fantastic, something I would never swop, but they are poor at communication. At least now we knew I wasn't actually dying and Sue could not have been happier. So much so, that she had me book a weeks' holiday, for her 68th birthday, in a farm cottage in Cornwall.

The South West coastal path was something we had started to do a week or so every year for the last three years. We loved the area and quite honestly it is, after all the travelling we have done - the cruises around the South China Sea, the Baltic, road trips round the USA - all we wanted to do from now on. Amazing isn't it? Sue wouldn't be doing the stupid hiking. She would walk our little dog on the beaches, do the shopping and the cooking and rescue the idiot when he was exhausted or actually reached the planned destination for the day. It was sublime. It was also the first week of the 2020 lock down! We arrived the day before it started, but we were self isolating! Having a nice week. On our final day Sue picked me up at the National Trust carpark at Crackington in the evening, now closed and unmanned since the pandemic. Sue is nothing if not reliable. We had a nice evening and, holiday over, we returned home the next day.

On the 21st of May we went to bed and had a "nice time", like you do when you are in love. Perhaps not as athletic as when we were 19 but tender and passionate still. But when Sue woke the following morning she felt confused and as if in a different dimension. She couldn't move or talk and knew she needed help, but couldn't summon any. I was not beside her - I was always up early - and it was only after I'd come up with a cup of tea, given her my usual stimulating bollocking for not getting up, and had a shower that my brain kicked in. I was back like lightning. "Christ Susie, I think you have had a stroke!" This wasn't part of our plan. I had all the illnesses, that was a given.

Role reversal was new to us both and Covid 19 was the first big hurdle. But within a few weeks a system of face to face visits was made possible. I had to wear protective clothing, a face mask and gloves and we were not allowed to touch and had to remain 2 meters apart. That didn't last longer than the staff leaving and closing the door. We were still lovers for goodness sake! Though I was crying like a cartoon baby. I never attended a "crying doesn't help" training scheme. Eventually after much physiotherapy, other treatments and a "Susan's best interests meeting" Sue was moved to a home where a system of Covid secure visits was again made possible. The second time, when we parted, as Sue was wheeled away, I said "I love you beauty". "I love you too" she replied. But the following day Sue was suffering with breathing difficulties and was rushed to A&E. In the middle of that night I received a telephone call from a nurse, to visit sharpish and came hot-foot on my motorbike to where she had been waiting for me, struggling to hang on. I held her hand and sobbed "Susie, Susie my lovely Susie", but she could do nothing more. So she died.

———————

Sue had joined me at the start of that last Bude to Crackington Haven section of our final holiday. We walked, with her dog Wilson, along Summerleaze beach, heading south. Parting company at the foot of the cliffs, which I had to climb as part of the footpath. It is hard to believe but we were as much in love as we were 50 years before. What a privilege! What a pleasure! With the writing of this book bringing us even closer. Each revealing how we felt about each other at particular moments in our evolution. Very revealing and cathartic.

At the top of the cliff is a memorial seat, so I took a moment. I looked for her and her companion Wilson. Watching them walk across the beach, she was easy to spot in her bright yellow 'Spider' jacket. A lovely garment that complimented her glowing character. I watched her all the way up the hill on the other side, with a warm glow in my heart, until they were gone and out of sight.

It is my treasured, abiding memory of her, and it will stay with me forever.

Clive and Sue 1973